*Jewish Monotheism
and Christian
Trinitarian Doctrine*

Jewish Monotheism and Christian Trinitarian Doctrine

A Dialogue by

Pinchas Lapide & Jürgen Moltmann

Translated by Leonard Swidler

FORTRESS PRESS   Philadelphia

Library of Congress Cataloging in Publication Data

Lapide, Phinn E   1922–
     Jewish monotheism and Christian trinitarian doctrine.

     Translation of Jüdischer Monotheismus, christliche Trinitätslehre.
          1. Judaism—Relations—Christianity—Addresses, essays, lectures.   2.   Christianity and other religions —Judaism—Addresses, essays, lectures.   I.   Moltmann, Jürgen, joint author.   II.   Title.
     BM535.L2913   261'.26   80–8058
     ISBN 0–8006–1405–4

31784

JUL 16 1981

8528G80   Printed in the United States of America   1–1405

Contents

On May 22, 1978, an extraordinary parish convocation took place in the village of Niefern bei Pforzheim, West Germany. Pastor C. J. Heinemann-Grüder had invited the observant Jewish theologian and professor Dr. Pinchas Lapide, living in Frankfurt, and the Protestant theology professor Dr. Jürgen Moltmann from Tübingen to speak about one of the oldest and most difficult problem-complexes dividing Jews and Christians, namely, Jewish monotheism and the Christian doctrine of the Trinity. The lectures and discussion which followed were full of surprises. The questions directed to both of the speakers were straightforward and frank and prompted responses which were honest and openhearted. Where many participants had expected to find yawning chasms, they found bridges instead. Where one expected a lack of understanding, there was in fact understanding. Both the participants and the speakers returned home more thoughtful than before. Consequently the speakers have raised again in these pages the questions which seemed important to them and have attempted to find answers which invite the inquirers to search for a common path.

Foreword

Leonard Swidler

There is something new under the sun, something which did not exist already in ancient days, at least not west of the Indus Valley. This new thing is interreligious dialogue. Only in present times has the constellation of circumstances come about that allows it to occur.

At the first level interreligious dialogue is a dialogue, that is, a conversation on a common subject between two or more persons with differing views, the primary purpose of which is for each participant to learn from the other so that he or she can change. In the religious sphere in the past, we came together to discuss with those differing with us, for example, Christians with Jews, either to defeat an opponent, or to learn about an opponent so as to more effectively deal with him, or at best to negotiate with him. If we faced each other at all, it was in confrontation—sometimes more openly polemically, sometimes more subtly so, but always with the ultimate goal of defeating the other, because we were convinced we alone had the absolute truth.

But that is not what dialogue is. Stated negatively, dialogue is *not* debate. In dialogue each partner must listen to the other as openly and sympathetically as he or she can in an attempt to understand the other's position as precisely and, as it were, as much from within, as possible. Such an attitude automatically includes the assumption that at any point we might find the partner's position so persuasive that if we would act with integrity, we would have to change our own position accordingly. That means that there is a risk in dialogue: we might have to change, and change can be disturbing. But of course that is the point of dialogue—change and growth. We enter into dialogue so that *we* can learn, change, and grow, not so we can force change on the *other*, as one hopes to do in debate—a hope which is realized in inverse proportion to the frequency and ferocity with which debate is entered into. On the other hand, because in dialogue *each* partner comes with the intention of learning and changing him- or herself, one's partner in fact will also change. Thus the alleged goal of debate, and much more, is accomplished far more effectively by dialogue.

We are here speaking of a specific kind of dialogue, an interreligious dialogue. To have such it is not sufficient that the dialogue partners discuss a religious subject. Rather, they must come to the dialogue as persons somehow significantly identified with a religious community. If I were neither a Jew nor a Christian, for example, I could not participate as a "partner" in a Jewish-Christian interreligious dialogue, though I might listen in, ask some questions for information, and make some helpful comments.

Because of this "corporate" nature of interreligious dialogue, and since the primary goal of dialogue is that each partner learn and change him- or herself, it is also necessary that interreligious dialogue be a two-sided project. Each participant must enter into dialogue not only with her partner across the faith line—the Christian with the Jew, for example—but also with her coreligionists, with her fellow Christians, to share with them the fruits of the interreligious dialogue. Only thus can the whole community eventually learn and change, moving toward an ever more perceptive insight into reality.

Let us reflect briefly on the circumstances which now make this new phenomenon of interreligious dialogue possible. First, however, by way of a prefatory remark it should be noted that these reflections provide only the briefest of outlines and hence, given the seriousness of the topics, will perforce raise a number of weighty questions without being able to discuss them adequately so as to arrive at a satisfactorily argued and documented resolution. Nevertheless, it is hoped that these brief comments will serve as a stimulus not to debate but to dialogue on these profound questions.

The new circumstance which now makes interreligious dialogue possible, at least for a significant, and growing, minority of religious believers today, is the spread of a nonabsolutized, dynamic view of truth. This new view of truth has come about in at least three different, but closely related, ways. They will be listed and then each will be briefly described.

1. Historicizing of truth: truth is deabsolutized and dynamized in terms of time, both past and future, with intentionality and action playing a major role in the latter.
2. Sociology of knowledge: truth is deabsolutized in terms of geography, culture, and social standing.
3. Limits of language: truth as the meaning of something and especially as talk about the transcendent is deabsolutized by the nature of human language.

1a. The historicizing of truth: Before the nineteenth century in Europe truth was conceived in quite an absolute, static manner. It was thought that if something was true at some time or other, it was always true. This understanding was usually applied to philosophical and theological statements of what the truth was. For example, if it was true for the Pauline writer to say in the first century that women should keep silence in the church, then it is always true; or if it was true for Pope Boniface VIII in 1302 to state in definitive terms that "we declare, state, and define that it is absolutely necessary for the salvation of all human beings that they submit to the Roman Pontiff," then it is always true.

In the nineteenth century many scholars came to perceive all statements about the truth of the meaning of something as being partially products of their historical circumstances. Those concrete circumstances helped determine the fact that the statement under study was even called forth, that it was couched in particular intellectual categories (for example, abstract Platonic or concrete legal language), literary forms (for example, mythic or metaphysical language), and psychological settings (for example, a polemic response to a specific attack). It was argued by these scholars that only by placing the truth statements in their historical *Sitz im Leben* could they be properly understood and that to express the same original meaning in a later *Sitz im Leben* one would require a proportionately different statement. Thus, all statements about the meaning of things were seen to be deabsolutized in terms of time.

1b. Later, especially with the work of thinkers like Max Scheler and Karl Mannheim, a corollary was added to this historicizing of knowledge; it concerned not the past but the future. These and other scholars also conceived of knowledge of truth as having an element of intentionality at the base of it, as being oriented ultimately toward action. They argued that we perceive certain things as questions to be answered and set goals to pursue certain knowledge because we wish to do something about those matters; we intend to live according to the truth, the meaning of things, that we hope to discern in the answering of the questions we pose, in gaining the knowledge we decide to seek. Thus, the truth of the meaning of things as stated by anyone is seen as deabsolutized by the action-oriented intentionality of the thinker-speaker.

2. The sociology of knowledge: As the statements of truth about the meaning of things were seen by some thinkers to be historically deabsolutized in time, so also starting in this century such statements were seen to be deabsolutized by the cultural, class (and so forth) standpoint of the thinker-speaker, regardless of time. Thus, a statement about the true meaning of things will be partially determined by the world view of the thinker-speaker. All reality was said to be perceived from the cultural, class, sexual (and so forth) perspective of the perceiver. Therefore, any statement of the truth of the meaning of something was seen to be "standpoint-bound," *standortgebunden,* as Karl Mannheim put it, and thus deabsolutized.

3. The limitations of language: Many thinkers have come to understand that all statements about the truth of things neces-

sarily can at most be only partial descriptions of the reality they are trying to describe. This is said to be the case because although reality can be seen from an almost limitless number of perspectives, human language can express things from only one, or perhaps a very few, perspectives at once. Whether this is the case concerning so-called scientific truths may be the subject of debate among some such scholars, but they are agreed that concerning statements about the truth of the meaning of things it is the case. The very fact of dealing with the truth of the "meaning" of something indicates that the knower is essentially involved and hence reflects the *Standortgebundenheit* of all such statements.

Moreover, the limited and limiting, as well as liberating, quality of language is especially seen when there is talk of the transcendent. By definition the transcendent is that which goes beyond our human experience. But we humans have only a human language with which to think and speak about that which we are persuaded exists beyond our experience. Hence, all statements about the transcendent are seen to be extremely deabsolutized and limited even beyond the limiting factor of *Standortgebundenheit*.

There were also other specific historical circumstances that helped to provide the setting that now makes interreligious dialogue possible, but the above three developments were important ideological elements in that setting. Even if all three were not present but at least one of them was, so that a deabsolutized view of truth began to emerge, then the necessary ideological component for interreligious dialogue would have been in place. Put in other words, a deabsolutized view of truth is a necessary but not sufficient cause of interreligious dialogue. Said in still another way, it is not possible to enter into interreligious dialogue if either partner has a completely absolutized view of truth. That further implies that a dialogue partner must be willing to engage in self-criticism of his or her own position. At the very least, one would have to be willing to complement one's view of the meaning of something with other views.

What then do persons with a deabsolutized view of truth who

wish to enter into interreligious dialogue do if their prospective partners hold an absolutized view of truth? Do they shrug their shoulders and walk away? Hardly. They must begin the conversation at whatever level possible in the hope (which has the support of experience) that with the slow building of personal trust and the addition of fresh information and insights, at least some of the absolutist partners will gradually, perhaps quite unconsciously, move toward a deabsolutizing of their views. Then real dialogue, the two-way, open conversation, will slowly happen. Before that there was only a prolegomenon to dialogue.

With the deabsolutized view of the truth of the meaning of things we come to face with the specter of relativism, which is the opposite pole of absolutism. If many no longer view absolutism as tenable, in light of the intellectual developments outlined above, a total relativism is also perceived as untenable because it logically would lead to an atomizing solipsism (self-alone-ism) which would stop all discourse, all statements to others (we know what happens to people who talk only to themselves).

There are several things that can be done to avoid that abyss, including the following two: One, besides striving to be as accurate and fair as possible in our gathering and assessing of information, submitting it to the critiques of our peers and other thinkers and scholars, we need also to dredge out, state clearly, and analyze our own presuppositions—but this is a constant, ongoing task. However, even in doing this we will be operating from a particular *Standort.* Therefore, we need, secondly, to complement our constantly critiqued statements with statements from different *Standörter.* That is, we need to engage in dialogue with those who have differing cultural, philosophical, social, religious viewpoints so as to strive toward an ever fuller perception of the truth of the meaning of things.

In interreligious dialogue, if we are serious and patient enough, we should at length be able to perceive below the public affirmation of others, which may be at odds with our own, their core concern, their intentionality. We can do this by utilizing sociology of knowledge. If we then also apply it carefully to ourselves and discern our own core concern, our own intentionality, we might then be in a position to reformulate our own concern in such a way as to also bring it closer to the core concern in the other. Thus, as Gregory Baum has noted, "Without reprehensible compromise the consensus has been widened: truth becomes more universal."[1]

How in the concrete can we engage in this new thing under the sun? The following are some basic ground rules of interreligious dialogue that must be observed if dialogue is actually to take place. These are not theoretical rules but ones that have been learned from hard experience.

First, each participant must come to the dialogue with complete honesty and sincerity. No false fronts have any place in dialogue.

Secondly, each participant must assume a similar complete honesty and sincerity in the other partner. Not only will the absence of sincerity prevent true dialogue from happening, so also will the absence of the assumption of the partner's sincerity. In brief: no trust, no dialogue.

Thirdly, each participant must define herself. Only the Jew, for example, can define from the inside what it means to be a Jew. The rest can only describe what it looks like from the outside. Moreover, because dialogue is a dynamic medium, as each participant learns, she will change and hence continually deepen, expand, and modify her self-definition as a Jew—being careful to remain in constant dialogue with her fellow Jews. Thus it is mandatory that each dialogue partner herself define what it means to be an authentic member of her own tradition.

Fourthly, each participant must come to the dialogue with no hard-and-fast assumptions as to where the points of disagreement are. Rather, each partner should not only listen to the other partner with openness and sympathy but also attempt to agree with the dialogue partner as far as is possible while still maintaining integrity with his own tradition; where he absolutely can agree no further without violating his own integrity, precisely there is the real point of disagreement—which most often turns out to be different from the point of disagreement that was falsely assumed ahead of time.

Fifthly, dialogue can take place only between equals, *par cum pare,* as Vatican II puts it. This means that not only can there be no dialogue between a skilled scholar and a "person in the pew" type (at most there can be only a garnering of data in the manner of an interrogation) but also there can be no such thing as a one-way dialogue. For example, Jewish-Christian discussions begun in the 1960s were mainly only prolegomena to interreligious dialogue. Understandably and properly, the Jews came to these exchanges only to teach the Christians, although the Christians came mainly to learn. But if authentic interreligious dialogue between Christians and Jews is to occur, then the Jews must also come mainly to learn; only then it will be *par cum pare.*

Lastly, although interreligious dialogue must occur with some kind of "corporate" dimension to it, that is, the participants must be involved as members of a religious community—for example, qua Jews or Christians—it is also fundamentally true that it is only *persons* who can enter into dialogue. But a dialogue among persons can be built only on personal trust. Hence it is wise not to tackle the most difficult problems in the beginning but rather to approach first those issues most likely to provide some common ground, thereby establishing the basis of human trust. Then, gradually, as this personal trust deepens and expands, the more thorny matters can be undertaken. Thus, as in learning we move from the known to the unknown, so in dialogue we proceed from commonly held matters—which, given our mutual ignorance resulting from centuries of hostility, will take us quite some time to discover fully—to discuss matters of diagreement.

In conclusion it should be noted that there are at least three phases in interreligious dialogue. In the first phase we unlearn misinformation about each other and begin to know each other as we truly are. In phase two we begin to discern values in the partner's tradition and wish to appropriate them into our own tradition. For example, in the Catholic-Protestant dialogue Catholics have learned to stress the Bible, and Protestants have learned to appreciate the sacramental approach to Christian life, both values traditionally associated with the other's religious community. If we are serious, persistent, and sensitive enough in the dialogue, we may at times enter into phase three. Here we together begin to explore new areas of reality, of meaning, of truth, of which neither of us had even been aware before. We are brought face to face with this new, unknown-to-us dimension of reality only because of questions, insights, probings produced in the dialogue. We may thus dare to say that patiently pursued dialogue can become an instrument of new revelation.

In the following dialogue between Pinchas Lapide and Jürgen Moltmann we have an example of what an authentic interreligious dialogue can produce: exciting new insights into the meaning of reality that neither alone had more than an inkling of. As a result of this dialogue each is more profoundly a Jew and a Christian, respectively, but at the same time each is profoundly closer to each other.

NOTES

1. Gregory Baum, *Truth Beyond Relativism: Karl Mannheim's Sociology of Knowledge* (Milwaukee: Marquette University Press, 1977), p. 70.

Foreword

Jacob B. Agus

The Lapide-Moltmann dialogue is an excellent illustration of the kind of interreligious explorations that are now going on throughout the world. The reader senses an air of mutual discovery and enrichment. The goal of "converting" others to one's own faith turns out to be irrelevant to the discussion, which is so truly worthwhile within its own realm of discourse. A new dimension is added to the experience of religion—the understanding in love of the religion of one's neighbor. And once this dimension is opened, it becomes clear that a living faith implies the obligation to open one's mind and heart to a sincere perception of the faiths of others. We tend to think of religions as living organisms, which are allergic to one another. But essentially mature religions are also spiritual entities, which seek openness and universal validity.

Professor Swidler points out the several ways whereby religions are deabsolutized in the modern world. His points are well taken. I should add that religious experience in itself includes an awareness of one's finitude as well as an apprehension of the infinity of the mystery of being. All religious teachers speak of humility as the unvarying preparation for and consequence of the nuclear religious experience. The Book of Numbers lists this quality as the primary characteristic of the master prophet, Moses. Isaiah is made aware that his lips are unclean, Jeremiah pleads that he is but a "boy," and Micah sums up the essence of faith in the superb phrase "to do justice, to love mercy, and to walk humbly with the Lord thy God." Jesus' critique of the Pharisaic establishment of his day focuses on this theme: piety without humility is hypocrisy. The Talmud adds that the Lord says of whoever is proud of heart, "I and he cannot dwell together."[1] To know that one does not know the fullness of God's will is the beginning and end of piety.

The nuclear religious experience deepens one's feeling of unworthiness even as it provides a thrust of reassurance and an intense awareness of love: "Underneath are the everlasting arms," and "I love you, says the Lord."[2] Love issues in a hunger for more love, in the longing to make oneself a "dwelling place for his Presence." In biblical Hebrew, love and the quest of understanding are denoted by the same word, *yodea*. While this longing cannot be converted into a permanent possession, it is in itself the proof of genuine love. Hence, the knowledge of nonpossession of the Divine is an integral dimension of the living pulsation of faith. And this awareness is a spur to the infinite quest of truth.

To be sure, there are ample opportunities within each of the great historical faiths to direct this hunger for love and understanding into productive channels. Within Judaism, the learning of Torah is a supreme commandment, and within Christianity, it is truth that makes one free (John 8:32). It is possible for Jews, Christians, and Muslims to study respectively their own rich traditions and to ignore the wisdom and insights that abound in other faiths. But history has demonstrated that such self-limitations have led to horrendous misrepresentations, distortions, and full-blown mythologies, bringing in their train disastrous consequences for humankind as a whole. In the absence of a living dialogue, the ninth of the Ten Commandments is certain to be transgressed.

We live today in an apocalyptic age. The self-destructive phase of the *eschaton* is a real possibility. Humankind is at the crossroads between the pathway leading to Armageddon and the one pointing toward the Kingdom of God. The duty to think in terms of humankind as a whole devolves upon all of us. Tribalism is today's "original sin." We can no longer afford to seek our total fulfillment by building ever higher the walls of our own "City of God." We have to learn to live within two worlds at one and the same time—the world of our own particular tradition and that of humanity, which is still struggling to be born. These two worlds cannot be kept apart in separate compartments of our minds. For, as Jesus put it, the command to love God with all our heart and mind is one with the command to love our neighbors as we do ourselves.

In the interfaith dialogue, the universal dimension of faith is experienced in all concreteness as a field of tension between historic traditions, not merely as a set of pale abstractions. Only in this way can the social momentum of the many reinforce the prophetic visions of the few and generate the emotional energy that the building of God's Kingdom requires.

The approach of Lapide to the Jewish-Christian dialogue is unique. He accepts the resurrection of Jesus as a historic occurrence, which galvanized the primitive Jewish-Christian community and produced that immense enthusiasm which no earthly obstacle could resist. The empty tomb of Golgotha and the appearance of the crucified one to 530 individuals, by his count, formed the living seed of a "God-willed" ecclesia, designed for the salvation of humankind.

I feel that it is not miracles in the sense of breaches in the dikes of physical laws that create religions. Rather, it is religions in the sense of ways of relating to the Divine Being that generate myths and miracles. Already the tenth-century philosopher Saadia maintained that miracles cannot prove true that which is either irrational or immoral ("Beliefs and Opinions" 3.8). A fresh way of sensing the dependence of this world upon the mystery of transcendence makes all things seem new and wondrous. It sets into motion a reexamination of the sacred tradition on the one hand and an air of expectancy in regard to a future release from troubles. Saadia interprets Jeremiah's prediction of a "new covenant" in this sense, of the reacceptance of the Torah itself with heart entire. It becomes impossible and in truth irrelevant to separate with certainty fact from fancy. Saadia and Maimonides point out that the people of Israel did not believe Moses on account of the miracles he performed but rather because they were persuaded that his message was true, indeed a "fulfillment" of an ancient promise (Saadia, "Beliefs and Opinions" 3.8; Maimonides' Code, *Mada* 8).

In the Jewish world of the first century, there were pietists who were reputed to be amazing wonder-workers. The revival of the dead was in fact a miracle that was mentioned rather frequently (*'Abod. Zar.* 10b; *Tanna debe Eliyahu* 5; "Of Messiah Reviving the Dead," *Pirqe R. El.* 32). Jesus refers to the disciples of the Pharisaic sages as performers of various miracles (Luke 11:19). But such attainments did not lift their possessors out of the ranks of humanity. Characteristic is the story told in the Talmud of the relation of Rabban Yohanan Ben Zakkai to Rabbi Hanina Ben Dosa:

The son of Yohanan got sick. He sent messengers to Hanina asking him to pray for his son's recovery. Hanina's prayer saved the life of the boy. Said Yohanan's wife to him: "You are Hanina's teacher. Why did not your prayer help?" Said Yohanan, "I am like an official in the King's palace, Hanina is like a servant."[3]

Standing as I do within the Jewish philosophical tradition, I recognize only miracles in the realm of the human mind and heart, great surges of moral fervor and leaps of the spirit that expand the horizon of humanity and its culture. The ferment of ideals, sentiments, and visions is the open frontier of evolution. The miracle of the Exodus from Egypt was the birth of freedom, faith, and courage in the hearts of a slave population. They dared to cross the Red Sea, while their pursuers, heavily armed mercenary soldiers, hesitated, held back, and when they finally entered the waters against their better judgment, they were defeated by the mud and the tides.

So I see the miracles of Scripture as metaphors of the immense potential for good of the human spirit. In all of creation, there is no greater demonstration of God's grace than the minds and hearts of rare sages and saints. These are the "wonders and favors" that God bestows upon us "every day, morning, evening, and afternoon."[4] His "chosen" spirits, though raised in diverse traditions, enrich the lives of all of us. So the sagas of the Incarnation and the Resurrection belong peculiarly to the Christian faith, while the teaching and life of Jesus challenge and inspire all people of faith.

No miracles of decisive importance stand alone, to be either affirmed or denied. They are integral elements of a living tradition.

From a practical standpoint, the Resurrection of Jesus is, for most Christians, a symbolic demonstration of his unique status as being both God and man, the only begotten Son of God. The evolution of ideas in the first century of our era, occasioned by the transfer of beliefs from the Hebraic to the Hellenic realm of discourse, cannot be duplicated in our day. The abyss between two ways of thinking about God was dug deep by the course of history.

Lapide accepts the basic axioms of Franz Rosenzweig in regard to the interaction of Christianity and Judaism. Jews are already "at the goal" of perfection, while Christians are charged with the task of bringing themselves and the world ever nearer to the Kingdom of God. The Hegelian roots of this conception belong outside the scope of this introduction. Its roots in popular Judaism are also undeniable. But in the Jewish philosophical tradition, this invidious distinction between the Torah-community and the rest of humankind has been transcended from time to time. In Maimonides' famous parable of the various sages of all religions, seeking to come close to the same King, the Talmudists are ranked lower than the philosophers (*Guide of the Perplexed* 3.51). In Halevi's image of the tree with three branches growing out of the divine seed, in the fullness of time the same seeds will reappear in all branches (J. Halevi, *The Kuzari* 4.23). Even in the nonphilosophical Midrashim there are references to "the renewal of Torah," or to a "new Torah" that will be manifested in the *eschaton* (*Tanna debe Eliyahu, Zuṭa* 20). The sectarians who produced the Book of Jubilees represented Torah as an exact copy of heavenly tablets, while the sages described Torah as the earthly, "decayed fruit of the Wisdom that is above" (Gen. Rab. 44).

Hence, perfection belongs to the eternal realm of ideas; Torah is an earthly representation of a heavenly reality. Deriving from divine inspiration, it is not free from the flaws and limitations of this material universe.

The Talmud states that "any one who eats without offering thanks to God betrays his mother and father"—his father being God, his mother being "the congregation of Israel" (*Ber.* 35b). Here, then, the share of the people in the molding of the tradition is acknowledged.

All Jewish scholars who address Christian lay audiences have been confronted again and again with the challenge, "Why don't you join us?" This question echoes the old belief that there can be only one true faith and the old disputations as to which faith is the *only* embodiment of the Divine Will.[5]

There is also the naive expectation that all humankind would live in perfect harmony and peace if only they all said Amen at the same time to the same litanies. But the tracks of history have been laid long before we were born. We are all creatures of historic forces. This fact implies both negative and affirmative conclusions. Our traditions, attitudes, myths, and rituals derive from the sources that are peculiar to our own particular position within the universal stream of history. The claim to be free of the trammels of the human condition is itself a sad commentary on the frailties of human nature. But God works within history his wonders to perform. And we are expected to respond to his call from whatever position we are in at any one time.

Lapide speaks of "a God-willed way of salvation," applying the phrase to Christianity and Islam as well as judaism. As I see it, I can only speak of a God-oriented way of life, lived "for the sake of his name in love."[6] Wandering in the wilderness as we do, we are called upon to reorient our life to him again and again, but we dare not assume we know and possess his will in all its fullness.

A Midrash states that "beside every blade of grass there stands an angel which beats it, saying, 'Grow.'" This too is the divine call to every human wherever he may be in the texture of history —to grow in the virtues of spiritual development.

Instead of searching for "the direction of a bridge between us," I suggest the image of an arc in an alternating current—it lights up precisely because of the difference in voltage. Our goal is to make pluralism fruitful, not to eliminate it.

Professor Moltmann's reference to Heschel's emphasis on the suffering of God is extremely interesting. Heschel expressed a poetic trend of Jewish symbolism that is reflected in talmudic as well as medieval sources. The Jewish philosophical tradition interpreted the passages referring to the pain of the Divine Presence as applying to "God as perceived by humans," not to "God in himself." Suffice it to note that the unity of God in Judaism, mystical or philosophical, does not exclude his being *in* man and *with* man. His Presence (Shekinah) visits the sick, shares in their anguish, endures the agonies of exile. At the same time, both philosophical and mystical Judaism exclude the notion of a suffering God, save as a metaphor for his compassion and sympathy.

A good case can be made for the thesis that primitive Christianity arose out of the mystical myths and symbols in ancient Judaism, for the rhetoric of Jewish mysticism comes closest to Christianity. As both scholars point out, Judaism and Christianity contain many and diverse strands of thought. All religious traditions are like flashlights, illuminating a cone of space and deepening the surrounding darkness. In our day, religious teachings are challenged as never before by the opposing tides of fundamentalist fanaticism on the one hand and militant nihilism on the other hand. The battlefront revolves round the central meaning of life itself, not along the peripheral texture of rites and symbols.

This dialogue reminds us that in the battle for the "things of God," we stand and fall together.

NOTES

1. *Sota* 5a.
2. Deut. 33:27; Mal. 1:2.
3. *Ber.* 34b.
4. The daily *'Amidah.*
5. Joseph Albo, *'Iḳḳarim* 1. 25, ed. I. Husik (Philadelphia: Jewish Publication Society).
6. Phrase in the opening paragraph of the *'Amidah.*

Jewish Monotheism

Pinchas Lapide

The people Israel grew up in the middle of a pagan world whose thinking, full of yearning and anxiety, peopled the groves and hills of antiquity with numberless guardian gods, who at bottom were nothing more than "scarecrows in a cucumber patch," as Jeremiah pitilessly pilloried them (Jer. 10:5). Nevertheless, they dominated a long-lived image of the world which rolled onward in powerful circles from cosmos to chaos and again back to cosmos, and then forward once again, ultimately returning to the original state in a goalless, pointless, and senseless manner. This earth, as a universal carousel of a historyless continuous cycle, in the ancient sagas was said to be the result of the obscene pairing of gods, the misbirth of monstrous heavenly Titans, whose priesthood demanded of their subjects the sacrifice of children, self-mutilation, and temple prostitution in order to eke out the brief course of their human existence.

"In the beginning God created heaven and earth." Here began the complete elimination of the power of all animal gods and idols; in fact, it emptied the heavenly bodies of all magic so that they, like all things in the universe, would be reduced to the instruments of the One God. This was the original conceptualization of evolution: a step-by-step upward-rising development of all earthly life, as it found expression in the immortal myth of the first week of creation. In one sentence the cosmos is explained as the order of nature providing humanity with a causal beginning, a continued life that is goal-conscious, and a final age that is full of hope. The word of the beginning was the end of the nightmares of darkness: "And there was light."

This explanation of Israel's, which within a millennium conquered the earth, is both "catholic" (for its world-embracing universality is as limitless as the gracious love of the Divine Creator) and "protestant" (with its powerful protest against the pagan world, which all too long divinized a portion of humanity as "gods" only to dehumanize others to the level of cattle). With this explanation there began the real world history of biblical civilization.

Polytheism is the religion of paganism—from the service of gods in early antiquity to the cult of idols in present-day Marxocracies—which constantly fixes its belief on created things so as to ascribe to this world's nature a divine omnipotence. Belief in One God is the foundation of Judaism, which behind the almost inexhaustible multiplicity of all perceivable reality sees the creation of the One God—which creation remains subordinated to God and to God alone. The Jew fundamentally is that one who can recognize the One God in all of God's raiments. The pagan on the other hand is that person who does not recognize God in God's numberless forms of appearance and consequently reveres the tangible things themselves.

With the passage of time a number of the great peoples of ancient cultures reached the level of henotheism, revering the one highest god as the chief of a heavenly pantheon full of lesser gods and goddesses. However, only the small people of the Jews was able to break through to the recognition of the true Oneness of God—thanks to the revelations which were granted it.

A thirst for unity would be the most laconic short formula into which one could compress the soul of Judaism: one and only is the Lord of creation, who created the universe—here is the source of the Hebraic concept of the universe—in which the Lord set the family of humanity, to whom the Lord gave common parents, one and the same destiny of humanity, and a common hope along the way for a redemption at the end of time.

"Why did God create only one Adam?" asks the Mishna.[1] It answers, "So that the heretic cannot say, 'In heaven there are many powers,'" for the fundamental unity of the whole human family—biologically, theologically, and teleologically—bears witness as much to the Oneness of the Creator as it does to the equal possibility of salvation for all of Adam's children. No image of God is salvationless or unloved! Those are the glad tidings of the Hebrew Bible.

Israel's monotheism, however, stems not so much from rational reflection as from the inextinguishable Thou experience which reveals the Lord of the universe as an unutterable "over-against" —that primary experience of the Exodus which became the cornerstone of the formation of the people of Israel. On the way out of slavery into the freedom of the desert everyone became a neighbor to the one nearest—even God. In the Second Book of Moses we read, "As a person speaks to a friend" (Exod. 33:11); thus did the dialogue between God and humanity develop. And on Mount Sinai: "I am your God who has led you out of the house of bondage" (Exod. 20:2). The leading out of Egypt—and it alone—say the Rabbis, gives God the right to say "I" and to lay upon humanity as "thou" the yoke of the reign of heaven.[2]

This I-thou experience of immediate relationship is so powerful, singular, and unique that it never allows the presentation of a plurality of principles or of a multiple personality of God to arise. In order to protect the Oneness of God from every multiplication, watering down, or amalgamation with the rites of the surrounding world, the people of Israel chose for itself that verse of the Bible to be its credo which to this very day not only belongs to the daily liturgy of the synagogue but also is impressed as the first sentence of instruction upon the five-year-old schoolchild.

This is the confession which Jesus acknowledged as the "most important of all the commandments"[3] and which is spoken by every child of Israel as a final word in the hour of death: "Hear, O Israel! The Lord our God is One" (Deut. 6:4). What the "Shema Israel" has meant for the inner life and survival of Judaism can only with difficulty be understood from without. As orthodox, liberal, or progressive as one might be in one's religiosity, the Oneness of God raises faith to a central height before which all other questions shrink to secondary ones. Whatever might separate the Jew on the fringe from the Jew at the center, the Oneness of the common God makes secure the oneness of religious consciousness.

This recognition of the Oneness of God matures with the prophets into a vision of the universal conversion of the world to the God of Israel—a view of the end of days which Martin Luther as well as Vatican II have accepted. In the words of the Herald of Israel: "Then, however, I will give pure lips unto the nations so that they all may call upon the name of the Lord and serve the Lord with one accord."[4] Pure lips, in a rabbinic exegesis, means that all of the nations without exception already for a long time have sought the One God, although they have often made use of strange circumlocutions in order to name God.

For indeed all human beings are fundamentally, as many Talmud masters along with Karl Rahner believe, "anonymous monotheists," whose service of God only needs a conceptual clarification. Even the last of the prophets returns to this fundamental thought: Thus said Malachi to the peoples of the world: "Do we not all have one Father? Has not the One God created us all?"[5]

Let the description of the death of Rabbi Akiba, who ended his life as a blood witness in a Roman torture chamber, serve as an illustration that this Oneness of God which suffers no duality became the touchstone of an endless row of Jewish martyrs. For the word *martyrdom* is indeed of Jewish origin and indicates nothing other than a "testimony" borne to the One God—in the sense of Isaiah: "You are my witnesses," says the Lord, "and my servant whom I have chosen" (Isa. 43:10 RSV)! Witness—if necessary even unto self-sacrifice. And thus it says in the Talmud:

> Only a few days passed and thus they seized Rabbi Akiba. At the hour when they led Rabbi Akiba out to his death it was precisely the time in which one read the "Shema"—the confession "Hear, O Israel"—and they tore his flesh from his body with iron combs. But he took the yoke of the reign of heaven upon him and

recited further the prayer. Then his disciples said to him, "Our
teacher, even until now?" But he answered them: "I have grieved
myself my whole life because of this verse, 'With your whole soul
shall you love God,' that is, even if someone takes your life. I
thought, when will the opportunity be given to me to fulfill it?
And now that the opportunity finally is offered, shall I not fulfill
it?" And he paused so along at the speaking of the word *"echad"*
(Oneness) that his soul breathed its last.[6]

This final word of the credo of Jesus and all his brothers and
sisters in the flesh, *echad*, which demythologizes and disdains
every polytheism, appears to this very day in every Jewish prayer
book in large-size bold print, for the final letter, daleth, can
purely optically only all too easily be misread as resh—which
would change "One God" to "another God" (*acher*), which according to a rabbinic opinion could call forth the end of the
world. The Oneness of God, which could be called Israel's only
"dogma," is neither a mathematical nor a quantitive oneness in
the sense of a rigid uniformity, but rather a living, dynamic Oneness out of whose inner essence the becoming-one of humanity
in the reconciliation of the all-embracing Shalom comes forth.

How nonstatic this all-oneness of God is is indicated already
by the tetragrammaton of the unutterable name of God, which
purely grammatically viewed is an active verbal form in the
future. And since the Hebraic concept of being denotes not a
simple existing, but rather much more an effective-being, a dy-
namically living–being, a co-being and a self-disclosing-being,
which all together is experienced as a process of becoming without pause, God's name already witnesses this to us: it pertains to
God's dynamic essence that it is becoming, and expressed itself
by in-the-world actions. Similarly active, open, and always new
are the three dimensions which the three Hebrew words of the
divine self-expression disclose: "I will be as the I will be" (Exod.
3:14). This concerns God's trustworthiness in helpful "co-being,"
God's being with us; it concerns the exclusiveness of God's standing by, which only God can guarantee, and the unmanipulatable
identity of God which is experienced ever anew, and whose forms

of appearance no one on earth can anticipate or restrict. All of these characteristics, which in the rational world of abstractions might split asunder into plurality, are reconciled in the Jewish world of belief into a wholeness of unity.

And thus the second article in the thirteen truths of faith compiled by Maimonides in medieval Spain reads, "I believe with complete conviction that the Creator—praised be God's name—is One, and that there is no Oneness which in any way is like unto God, and that God alone was, is, and will be our God."

Whoever perceptively reads between the lines here will note a polemic barb which is directed against the medieval understanding of the Trinity by the church. For the difference between gods and the One God is indeed not some kind of difference in number—a more miserable misunderstanding there could hardly be—but rather a difference in essence. It concerns a definition not of reckoning but rather of inner content; we are concerned not with arithmetic but rather with the heart of religion, for "one" is not so much a quantitative concept as a qualitative one. Two or more cannot be absolute. Two or more also cannot be timeless and eternal. If there are two or more, there can be no concept of omnipotence. Two or more must lead to a division of labor and to conflict; likewise, where the reception of "only two" is present, as by Zoroaster, the lordship will be divided between good and evil, with devastating effects in popular belief. For what the one bids, the other can forbid; what Zeus commands, Hera can sabotage—thus monotheism also becomes an indispensable presupposition of a mono-ethics.

"I am the Lord, there is no other; I form the light and create the darkness, I make well-being and create woe; I, the Lord, do all these things" (Isa. 45:6–7).

Only where a single God created a universe in order to place in it the family of humanity can a Decalogue demand universal obedience, can one and the same morality serve as a guideline for all mortals.

The God of Israel is the only One not because only the Lord

did and accomplished what all the heathen gods together did, but rather because the Lord is completely other than all of them are and because the Lord behaves differently than all of them do. The essence of God is completely opposed to that of the gods. The Lord is not for example simply more than they are or better than they are; the Lord stands incomparably over against them, for the Lord alone is the living One, the creating One, and the commanding One who proclaims what is commanded. To the Lord alone is it proper that humanity can truly serve God by the fulfillment of the Lord's moral demands.

From the Hebrew word *echad* we learn not only monotheism, not only that there is none outside of the Lord, but also that the Lord is One and therefore that the Lord cannot be viewed as something put together which would be divisible into various properties or attributes. Probably there has been no generation which has learned to understand so profoundly this primordial unity of the Creator and creation as has ours. The attempt of the Greeks to see the four fundamental elements as the foundation of the structure of the universe is well-known. The atomic theory of the philosopher Democritus is also known. All these and many others were milestones on the path to the scientific recognition of our century that all of the various elements are composed of the same tiniest particles. The difference exists only in the number and order in which they coalesce around a central point into tiny microcosms. And if our forebears still distinguished between two things upon which the structure of the world rested in dualistic fashion, namely, mass and energy, today it is taught that mass is nothing other than energy in coalesced form, and energy is mass extended outward. Thus step by step humanity attains an understanding of the unity in the building up of this unending, complex world—a fundamental unity, which accurately reflects the primordial unity of the Creator. The Jewish conception of this unity is however in no way statically conceived, which point must be stressed here again—in stark contradiction to Greek ontology. It is to be understood as dynamic rather than as a process. One does not speak of the "being one" (*Eins-Sein*) of God, but rather of the "union" (*Einung*) of God. In the words of Franz Rosenzweig in explaining the Shema Israel, "To confess God's unity—the Jew calls it: to unify God (*Gott einigen*). For this unity is as it becomes, it is Becoming Unity. And this becoming is enjoined on the soul and hands of man."[7]

This "union" (*Einung*) of God, which is much misunderstood, exists not only in the daily renewed affirmation of the divine unity in the multiplicity of appearances, but also in the reconciliation of all contradictory dualism, which pressed toward a loving "becoming one"—not only in the believing confession, but also in the realizing deed.

The unity of God, the Zohar[8] teaches us, depends upon the prayer of humanity. The fate of God is therefore, so to say, placed in the hands of the just ones, for only if the human person has fulfilled in itself this ardent union (*Einung*) can it say "Thou" to God and call upon God with the Lord's name. This union (*Einung*) of God is still on the way as long as multiplicity in the hearts of many of God's children has not yet attained "becoming one" (*Einswerdung*). To this messianic *unificatio*—the unity of all creatures under the lordship of the One God—the prophet Zechariah devotes his powerful concluding chapter, from which the prophecy of the Day of the Lord is taken to close the daily worship service, and whose words are echoed in 1 Cor. 15:28: "And God will be Ruler over the entire earth; on that day the Lord shall be the only One and the Lord's name the only one" (Zech. 14:9). In the words of Paul, "Then, however, the Son will also submit himself to the One to whom all things have submitted themselves, so that God may be all in all."

It is against this background of a radical, uncompromisingly understood monotheism that we must discuss the Jewish reactions to the Trinitarian doctrine of the church. The average Jew today considers the Trinity at best a kind of heavenly triumvirate, and at worst a tritheism which is reminiscent of a relapse into paganism, and nevertheless in both cases much too like polytheism to

still earn the name of monotheism. Not so those learned in the
Scriptures in Judaism, who already in the Talmud described the
Trinity of the church as *Shittuf*—in English, "bring together"—
a concept which Islam later as *Shirq* made the spearpoint of its
church critique.

Consequently the Koran, completely in the sense of the first
Tannaim, stated thus: "Speak: Your God is the only God, there is
no God outside of GOD. All those are infidels who maintain that
God is the third of three, whereas there is only One. If they do
not cease to declare this, a painful fate will be their portion."[9]

The Talmud fathers here are somewhat more mild-hearted than
the prophet Muhammad in that they maintained that this Trinitarian association (*Beigesellung*) indeed constricts pure monotheism but is no mortal sin, as is, for example, serving idols. Thus
we read in the tractate Sanhedrin of the Talmud that the same
behavior is attributed to the people of Israel—namely, at the
occasion of the worship of the golden calf at the foot of Mount
Sinai, from out of the mouths of the wavering ones in Israel it
was said, "These are your gods, Israel, who led you out of
Egypt" (Exod. 32:4). However, since they used the plural, says
the Talmud,[10] they therefore did not adore the calf alone, but
rather they bound together true worship of God with the worship
of idols. Thanks to this association (*Beigesellung*), which may
not be equated to an elimination of God, they were spared de-
struction. In this sense the Jews reckoned the Christians already
in the fourth century as "associators" (*Beigeseller*), who, as Paul
would have said, perceive the Godhead darkly through a dis-
torted mirror[11] or give worship to the creature rather than the
Creator,[12] but still do not have a clear vision of the One God.

Only in the ninth century did a serious exchange between
Christian and Jewish scholars take place, in the midst of which
Saadia Gaon, the head of the Talmudic academy at Sura in Baby-
lonia, could write: "I do not have . . . the common crowd in
mind which is only able to speak of a Trinity in a gross sense.
I do not wish to burden my book with rebuttals of these. . . .

33

I much rather wish to rebut the thinkers among them who imagine themselves to believe in a Trinity in a subtle thought pattern."[13]

After an implicit objection that the church fathers had dropped the letter *u* in order to construct once again from the word *Triunitas* the original *Trinitas* of Tertullian, Saadia declared to his fellow Jews that with educated Christians the situation is as if they said that they prayed to a burning-hot one, to a bright-shining one, and to a climbing-to-heaven one, without however composing the matter or explaining that it all pertains to one and the same fire. Here Saadia relies on the Augustinian doctrine of the Trinity in order to explain to his Jewish readers that the Trinity arises of the hypostatization of the three divine attributes of essence, life, and omniscience.[14] From this he draws the conclusion that all of this indeed contradicts the Jewish understanding of God, but that in spite of this the Christians should be acknowledged not as disguised idol worshipers but rather as genuine, if also odd, monotheists.[15] This view has found a home in broad circles of believing Judaism since the high Middle Ages.

One of the bases for this reconciliatory position, which Islam to this very day has not been able to partake of, is perhaps in the many triadic (in no way Trinitarian) traces which are to be found in Judaism. To begin with a most famous case in point: Why is it often written in the Bible, ask the Rabbis, "The God of Abraham, the God of Isaac, the God of Jacob"? Is there not only One God in heaven and on earth? And the Holy Scripture, which knows no lack, also knows no superfluous word. Therefore, why does it not say plainly and simply, "The God of Abraham, Isaac, and Jacob," instead of emphasizing a half-dozen times (as even Jesus in his dispute with the Sadducees repeated):[16] "The God of Abraham, the God of Isaac, and the God of Jacob"? The answer to this puzzle, which one might feel is a petty matter, came out gradually in a centuries-long debate.

The solution stated: The single Creator God of the whole world was experienced by the three patriarchs each in his own way, each according to his own destiny, each in his God-willed individuality. Abraham experienced the Lord as the God who leads out: out of the security of the safe Mesopotamia, which indeed was protected but was idolatrous, into the total uncertainty and lack of assurance of the Promised Land. Isaac, his son, experienced the Lord as the Redeemer God, who rescued him at the last moment on Mount Moriah from the sacrificial death by the knife of his own father. Jacob, the grandson, however, experienced God as the wrestling angel who struggled with him throughout the whole night until he could wring from him a blessing at dawn, a blessing for himself, and the new name Israel.

Israel, the wrestler against God—not the one who wrestles for God, but rather the stout battler who fights with his God—a quality which the ancestral father bequeathed along with his name to the whole people.

Thus it is right that it says in the Bible, "The God of Abraham, the God of Isaac, and the God of Jacob," for it concerns three different experiences of God which indeed fundamentally differ from each other. However, similarly legitimate and authentically genuine are the views of God of the synagogue, the church, and the mosque, the triunity of the monotheism of our present-day world.

Thus the recognition of religious pluralism came to Judaism already centuries ago, and the division into three slowly became a tradition in Judaism as well.

The mystics of the Cabala discovered a trace of the triad already on the first page of the Bible. "In the beginning God created heaven and earth, and the spirit of God hovered over the waters; then God said, 'Let there be light,' and there was light." Here stand the three (say the mystics, not normative Judaism): God's Self, God's Spirit, and God's Word, which in Hebrew is *Davar*, which later in Aramaic was called *Memra*—the two ancestors of the still later Greek *Logos*, as the first revelation of the One God.

Johannes Reuchlin, the student of two rabbis and a citizen of the city Pforzheim, who was the first Christian Cabala researcher, went one step further in that already in the second word of the Bible, *bara* "[and God] created," he wished to see a stenogram of the Trinity: beth as an abbreviation for *ben* ("the son"), resh for *ruach* ("the spirit"), and aleph for the Godhead itself (*elohim*).

Here also belongs the so-called *Kedusha*, or *Trishagion*, from Isa. 6:3 where the choir of angels sings, "Holy, holy, holy is the Lord of hosts; the entire earth is full of God's glory!" This doxology since time immemorial has been part of our daily morning prayer and the Prayer of Eighteen, which is spoken while standing. It is no wonder, therefore, that this so often repeated three-foldness of the holiness of God had led to a whole wave of quasi-trinitarian speculation in the fringe groups of Judaism, especially in connection with Ezek. 3:12, where it says, "And the Spirit lifted me up, and I heard behind me a large noise as the glory of the Lord raised itself up." The Spirit, the Glory, and the Lord's Self, say several of the mystics—there you have it: the three manifestations of the Godhead.

Something similar happened with the conclusion of the covenant at the foot of Sinai, where incredibly it is said of the Seventy Elders of Israel, "And they *saw the God* of Israel."[17] The Targum, the Aramaic translation of the Hebrew Bible, which at the time of Jesus was already widespread throughout the land, could not bring itself to literally repeat this verse, which contradicts all Jewish knowledge of God—and thus it used the circumlocution "And they saw *Kavod* (the Glory) of the *Shekinah* (the Presence) of the God of Israel."

Here Rabbi Eliezer gave a word of admonition which has become a basic hermeneutical rule in Judaism: "Everyone who exegetes or translates literally a word of the Bible is a liar. Everyone who adds something to it is, however, a blasphemer, for here he indeed makes of the God of Israel a Trinity, namely, Kavod, Shekinah, and the Godhead itself."[18]

Karl Rahner understands the world as God's self-communication, so that God meets us in three givens, as the Creator who gives God's Self to humanity; as the Redeemer who lets us understand this as grace; and as the Spirit whose Self gives us our yes to God. This understanding of the Trinity has an extraordinary parallel in a midrash to Exod. 3:14 where likewise the concern is with the self-communication of God in the form of the disclosing of the Lord's name. A midrash has God answer Moses, who had asked God's name, "I will always be named according to my works. . . . As *Elohim* I am the judging God; as Lord of Hosts I lead war against the impious; as *El-Shaddai* I am the God who condemns sins, and as the Tetragrammaton [which we Jews do not speak out loud] I am the God of love and mercy."[19] But most of all it is true that "I will be there as the I-decide-to-be-there" (Exod. 3:14), and no human mind may rob God's salvific action of even a fraction of an inch of God's unpredeterminable sovereignty.

Something similar was said by Rabbi Zalman Shneur of Ladi, the founder of the Lubavitcher dynasty, one of the pillars of Hasidism: "He is the Knowing One, the One Known, and the Knowledge. All these three form in God an indivisible unity." This is reminiscent of Karl Barth, who spoke of God as "the Revealer, the Revelation, and the Being-Revealed."

A final locus classicus in triadic thought in Judaism should be mentioned here—the theophany of Abraham at Mamre. In the words of Genesis 18, "And the Lord appeared to him at the grove of Mamre . . . and as he raised his eyes up and looked, behold, there stood before him three men. And when he saw them he ran toward them . . . and said, 'Lord, if I have found grace before your eyes, do not pass your servant by.' . . . Then they said to him, 'Where is Sarah, your wife?' . . . Then the Lord said to Abraham, 'Why does Sarah laugh? Should something be impossible with the Lord? I will come again at this time next year, and then Sarah shall have a son.'"

The transition from the number three of the men to the number One of God in this pericope is so frequent and so immediate that the number of rabbinical interpretations of this passage exceeds a dozen. Nevertheless, it appears clear to most of the exegetes that God is manifested here in a triad of men, or as one of the three men, which corresponds to a dynamic monotheism attempting to bring the manifoldness of the experience of God under a single roof. Particularly interesting here is the commentary of Rabbi Benno Jakob: "Then the Lord appeared to him . . . through 'men,' for the closer a human being is allowed to stand to God, the more human are the appearances of God."[20]

This same intention is also manifested in the *Sefirot* doctrine of the Cabalists, which perceives God only as a dynamic process between ten different levels of the Godhead. It is a doctrine of the manifestations of God which understands the unity of God as so far above human knowledge that human beings are able to meet their God only in a phenomenological multiplicity. This reminds me of a pastor in Bavaria who dared to unravel the Trinitarian formula so as to say in his church, "The Father *through* the Son *in* the Holy Spirit." One thing is clear: the whole rainbow of Jewish experiences of God is and remains in Judaism nothing other than a gallery of verbal images which neither are now nor ever have become stone-hard concepts on which one could build a putative pseudoknowledge of God, or indeed a fully articulated system. All these images without exception are a helpless stammering which at best is only on the way toward the unutterable, which, however, can neither now nor ever be theologized in fixed formulas of precise sequence or indeed in an accurate ordering of rank.

Thus can Haggai the prophet say in the name of God, "I am with you according to the word of the promise that I made you . . . and by my Spirit, who abides among you"[21]—without this statement's ever becoming a definition of the essence of God in Judaism.

We can assume that the Jew Jesus knew of a Trinity in a dogmatic sense just as little as the Jew Paul, who could say, "The Lord is the Spirit!"[22] whereby, in good Jewish fashion, the *Kyrios* is not yet separated from the *Pneuma*. And in the same epistle he is certain neither of the terminology nor of the sequence when he says, "The grace of the Lord Jesus Christ, and the love of God, and the fellowship of the Holy Spirit."[23] Here he appears rather to be speaking of a poetic triad, as faith, hope, and love in 1 Corinthians 13, rather than of a dogmatic Trinity, of which indeed the Jew Paul could have had no knowledge, since that came into the world only centuries after his death.

If Jesus answered the question about the greatest commandment with the Shema Israel (Mark 12:29), there is no lack of evidence in the Pauline writings witnessing to the fact that even the apostle to the Gentiles held true to the monotheism of his Lord: "The head of Christ, however, is God" (1 Cor. 11:3). "There is, however, only one God, the Father, from whom all things are and whose we are" (1 Cor. 8:6). "There is, however, only one and the same God who works all things in all" (1 Cor. 12:6). "One God and Father of all, who is above all and by all and in all" (Eph. 4:6). "All things are yours, you, however, are Christ's, Christ, however, is God's" (1 Cor. 3:22–23).

Whoever knows the development of the history of dogma knows that the image of God in the primitive church was unitary, and only in the second century did it gradually, against the doctrine of subordinationism, become binary. For the church fathers such as Justin Martyr, Irenaeus, and Tertullian, Jesus is subordinated to the Father in everything, and Origen hesitated still to direct his prayer to Christ, for, as he wrote, that should properly be to the Father alone. At this point he referred to the words of Jesus in the Gospel of John: "The Father who has sent me is greater than I."[24]

The total picture which arises from history is almost like an arithmetic progression: In the first century God is still monotheistic in good Jewish fashion. In the second century God becomes two-in-one; from the third century on God gradually becomes threefold. Only in the fourth century, however, does the elevation of the Holy Spirit to a special hypostasis with its own value take place. Moving from the "Binity" of the primitive church, in the year 381 at the Second Council of Constantinople, against the heavy resistance of a whole series of church fathers, the divine triunity of the full doctrine of the Trinity is canonized. How uncertain the linguistic foundation of the personification of the Holy Spirit is was witnessed to already by Jerome: "The Spirit, however, is feminine gender in Hebrew, masculine in Latin, but neuter in Greek."[25]

Still in the fifth century the so-called *Pneumatomachoi*, as they called themselves, who did not wish to grant to the Spirit the same equality and essence as between the God-Father and the God-Son, jeered that the new dogma would make the Father-God in reality a grandfather of the Holy Spirit.

"Distinguished but undivided, bound together in otherness, one in three: that is the Godhead and the three are one."[26] When one reads this credo of Gregory of Nazianzus (from January 6, 381), which one still hears today in the church liturgy, one can only regret with Hans Küng "the unbiblical, very abstractly constructed speculation of the School tractates" as well as "the Hellenization of the Christian primordial message by Greek theology"[27]—and agree with him when he expresses "the genuine concern of many Christians and the justified frustration of Jews and Muslims in trying to find in such formulas the pure faith in one God." It was during the bloody intra-Christian religious wars of the fourth and fifth centuries, when thousands upon thousands of Christians slaughtered other Christians for the sake of the Trinity, that—as biblical research has long since proven—the Trinitarians edited their notorious *Comma Johanneum* into the First Epistle of John: "For there are three who give witness in heaven, the Father, the Word, and the Holy Spirit, and the three are one."[28]

Goethe may have had in mind this passage, which was missing from Luther's original translation of the Bible, when he said to Eckermann on January 4, 1824: "I believe in God and in nature, and in the victory of the noble over the evil. But that was not enough for the pious soul; I should also believe that three are one and one are three. But that contradicted the quest of my soul for truth; also, I could not see that I would be helped by it even in the least."

Claus Westermann appeared to have a similar opinion when recently in a collection of essays he wrote of Christian theology: "The question of the relationship of the persons of the Trinity to one another and the question of divinity and humanity in the person of Christ as a question of the ontic relationships could only arise when the Old Testament had lost its significance for the early church. The christological and Trinitarian questions structurally correspond to the mythological questions into the relationship of the gods to one another in a pantheon."[29]

F. C. Conybeare had already shown in 1901 that in all the manuscripts and copies of Eusebius, which were written down before the Council of Nicea took place in 325, the Trinitarian formula in the conclusion of Matthew is missing.[30] The most likely original text of the original mission command of Jesus has been reconstructed by David Flusser on the basis of rabbinic analogies and from the manuscripts of the library of Caesarea: "Go forth and make all nations disciples in my name, teaching them to hold to everything which I have commanded you."[31]

In view of the present-day significance of the doctrine of the Trinity for Christian belief, I can without difficulty agree with the claim of Karl Rahner that "the Christians, despite all their orthodox confessions of the Trinity, in their religious living are almost only 'monotheists.' One might dare to claim that even if the doctrine of the Trinity had to be eliminated as false, the great majority of religious writings could remain almost unchanged."[32]

If that is so, is it not time to take seriously the call of the General Synod of the Netherlands Reformed Church, which recommends a rethinking of the dogma of the Trinity? In the words of the Dutch, "On the Jewish side, an increasingly strong emphasis was laid on this unity [of God] through the course of the centuries, along with the development of the growing resistance to the ecclesiastical teaching of the Trinity, which was always misunderstood by the Jews, and incidentally also by Islam, as polytheism. Certainly the church must investigate how far the church itself is jointly guilty for the rise of these misunderstandings through the formulations in which this doctrine was gradually crystallized and presented."[33]

As a Jew, may I in this connection also refer to the Psalms and the Book of Proverbs, where in urgent and repeated fashion the fear of the Lord as the beginning of all wisdom is praised? This fear also means, however, a humble shyness in face of the holiness of God, a shyness from an all-too-express naming of the Lord's name, but above all a shyness from wishing to decipher precisely the inscrutable God of the Bible, to define or indeed to fix God in writing.

It is true that the manifold is needed for the one-becoming, that God could not practice gracious love if God's manifestations and ways of revelation were not dynamic and manifold. But it is just as true that no picture language of the Bible can grasp God's essence, that all dogmatic statements about the *Deus absconditus,* the inscrutable, hidden God, must bow before the words of the prophet which in the name of God admonish us all: " 'Is it to inquire of me that you come? As I live,' says the Lord God, 'I will not be inquired of by you.' "[34] Whereby God, the Lord of us all, on the lips of Moses, the prophets, and Jesus of Nazareth remained always only the one, only, and indivisible God of Israel.

Professor Moltmann also appears to be of this opinion; otherwise he would not have recently been able within the context of an ecumenical speech in Lausanne under the title "Ein Zurück gibt es nicht mehr!" ("There Is No More Return!") to say: "Fundamentally there are not two peoples of God, an old and a new one. As God is one, so also is God's people one."[35]

To that I can say with a full heart yes and amen.

NOTES

1. *M. Sanh.* 4. 5.
2. For a presentation of the rabbinical interpretations of Exod. 20:2, see Nechama Leibowitz, *Studies in the Shemoth* (Jerusalem 1976), part 1, pp. 303ff. (Amer. ed. New York: Phillip Feldheim, 1976).
3. Mark 12:29 and pars.
4. Zeph. 3:9.

5. Mal. 2:10.

6. Ber. 61b.

7. Franz Rosenzweig, *The Star of Redemption*, trans. William W. Hallo (New York: Holt, Rinehart and Winston, 1970), pp. 410–11.

8. See especially *Zohar* 1. 44b and 1. 53b.

9. Sura 5. 76.

10. *Sanh.* 63a; *Sipre Deut.* 43; *Mek. Mish.* 17.

11. 1 Cor. 13:12.

12. Rom. 1:25.

13. Saadia Gaon, *Emunot-we-Deot* 2. 5; cf. D. Kaufmann, *Geschichte der Attributenlehre* (Amsterdam 1967), pp. 38ff.

14. Ibid.

15. Of his famous disputation with the convert Paulus Christianus, which took place in Barcelona in 1263, Nahmanides (Rabbi Moses Ben Nahman of Gerona) wrote: "I asked Fra Pablo what the Trinity was . . . and he answered, 'Wisdom, Will, and Power.' Upon which I said: 'I too confess that God is wise and not foolish, that his will does not change, and that he is powerful and not weak. But the term *Trinity* is clearly an error. . . . For he, his wisdom, his will, and his power are one. . . . Following the Trinitarian line of reasoning one ought to speak of a Fourfoldness, for God, his wisdom, his will, and his power make four . . . one could even speak of a Fivefoldness if one added his aliveness. . . .' Whereupon Fra Pablo stood up and said he believed in the Unity which nevertheless encompassed the Trinity. But this, he maintained, was an unfathomable mystery, which not even the angels and the princes of heaven understood" (*Milchemet Choba* [Constantinople 1710], 13a).

16. Matt. 22:32.

17. Exod. 24:10.

18. Rabbi Eliezer, *Midrash ha-Gadol*, ed. S. Schechter (London 1902), on Exod. 24:10; cf. *Kiddushin* 49a.

19. *Exod. Rab.* 3. 6 on Exod. 3:14.

20. Rabbi Benno Jakob, *Genesis* (Berlin 1934), p. 437.

21. Hag. 2:5.

22. 2 Cor. 3:17.

23. 2 Cor. 13:14.

24. John 14:28.

25. Jerome "In Isaiam 40:9–11."

26. Gregory of Nazianzus, Migne, *PG* 36. 345 D.

27. Hans Küng, "Antwort an meine Kritiker," *Frankfurter Allgemeine Zeitung*, 22 May 1976.

28. 1 John 5:8.

29. Claus Westermann in *Theologie, was ist das?* ed. G. Picht (Stuttgart 1977), p. 50.

30. Matt. 28:18–20.

31. David Flusser, "The Conclusion of Matthew in a New Jewish-Christian Source," *Annual of the Swedish Theological Institute* 5 (1967): 110–20.

32. Karl Rahner, "Bemerkungen zum dogmatischen Traktat 'De Trinitate,'" *Schriften zur Theologie*, 5th ed. (Einsiedeln, Zurich, and Cologne 1967), 4:105.

33. "Israel und die Kirche: Eine Studie im Auftrag der Generalsynode der Niederländischen Reformierten Kirche" (Zurich 1961), p. 16.

34. Ezek. 20:3.

35. Jürgen Moltmann, "Ein Zurück gibt es nicht mehr!" as published in *Publik-Forum* 15 (22 July 1977): 14.

The Christian Doctrine of the Trinity

Jürgen Moltmann

By the connection of "monotheism" with Judaism and the "doctrine of the Trinity" with Christianity, obviously the difference between Jews and Christians in their understanding of God is supposed to be indicated: Judaism is represented then as "a monotheistic religion," while Christianity, in any case according to its traditional dogma, teaches a Trinitarian faith. In fact the Jew does pray daily, "Hear, O Israel, the Lord our God, the Lord is One," and Christian worship services still begin, "In the name of the Father and of the Son and of the Holy Spirit." But is the Jewish understanding of God therefore to be called "monotheistic" in the sense of philosophical monism? And does not Christian faith confess the tri-*une* God? The confession of the exclusivity of the "only" God need not be identical with the monistic concept of the "one" God.

Since Adolf von Harnack it is often said that the Christian doctrine of the Trinity, like all theological speculation, first arose under the influence of the philosophical Logos doctrine.[1] Therefore it is alien to Jesus' simple gospel of the merciful Father-God and the infinite value of the individual soul. But is that true? To be sure, in the Platonic and Neoplatonic philosophical schools there were triadic speculations on the absolute, and later Christian theology did in fact take thought categories for the Trinity out of Neoplatonism. But in the first centuries Aristotelianism was much more influential in the Greek cultural area. In the twelfth book of the Metaphysics Aristotle put forth "philosophical monotheism" of the one, simple, unmoved, apathetic, immortal, divine Being. The entire world had a monarchic constitution of being: one God, one law, one world.[2]

Judaism took over concepts of this philosophical monotheism and monarchism just as did Christianity as they both moved into the Greek and Roman culture area. What, however, has the authentic belief in God of Israel to do with the philosophical monotheism of Aristotle? And what distinguishes the Christian conception of the triune God from the divine One of the Aristotelian world monarchy?

To express the matter simply and directly, the concept of Jews and Christians is to be distinguished from the God of Aristotle through the historical experience of the *passion and the suffering of their God*. This experience creates a community of the two over against the apathetic God of the philosophers. And this community reaches deeply into their understanding of God, so deeply that I would like to try to trace the Christian doctrine of the Trinity back to its Hebraic and Jewish roots and develop it in harmony with the Jewish experience of God.

In this I am reckoning that there is no more *the* Jewish understanding than there is *the* Christian understanding. Rather, on the basis of the Jewish primordial experience there is a series of possibilities, and likewise also on the basis of the Christian primordial experience there is a series of possibilities. In this series of possibilities there fortunately are agreements, which appear shocking to those who at one time dogmatized only one of the possibilities.

Of what do we think when we hear the names of the triune God: Father, Son, and Holy Spirit? What notions do we connect with the Trinitarian concept of God, and with what experiences are our notions connected? A speculation?

Many Christians cross themselves when the triune God is mentioned. When the community is blessed in the name of the triune God it is customary to make the sign of the cross with the blessing hand. If people are baptized in the name of the triune God, then according to Paul they are buried with Christ into their death in order to live with the Risen One. In medieval pictures the so-called chair of grace often depicts the Trinity so that the Father sits on the throne of glory and lifts up the horizontal bar of the cross on which the dead Son hangs and the Holy Spirit in the form a dove descends from the face of the Father onto the bowed head of the crucified Son.

What is presented here in this fashion in pictures and in gestures shows that the Trinitarian concept of God was developed out of the understanding of the crucified Christ. According to Immanuel Kant, concepts without understandings are "empty." The understanding of the Trinitarian concept of God is the Christ crucified on Golgotha. Conversely, according to Kant, our understandings without concepts are "blind." Consequently the belief in the crucified Christ without the doctrine of the Trinity remains ununderstandable. The doctrine of the Trinity is nothing other than the conceptual framework needed to understand the story of Jesus as the story of God. The doctrine of the Trinity is the theological short summary of the story of the passion of Christ. With it we grasp the story of the passion of Christ as the story of divine passion. How far in this connection, however, is it necessary to speak of this self-distinguishing of God in the divine persons of the Father, Son, and Holy Spirit? Is there a preparation in the Old Testament and is there a correspondence in Jewish thought for this experience of the divine passion and for the perception of the self-distinguishing of God revealed therein?

Abraham Heschel[3] was the first who worked his way back through the forms of philosophical monotheism, which had been taken up by Jewish philosophers of religion in Europe as well, all the way to the original Jewish experience of God. In coming to terms with Cohen, Natorp, Spinoza, and Maimonides he broke through the philosophical axiom of the essential apathy of the divine nature and called the theology of the Old Testament prophets a "theology of divine pathos."[4]

In God's pathos the Almighty One goes out of Self and into

the people of God's choice. In God's pathos God becomes a covenant partner of this people. God is defined. God is committed. God is made callable. Therefore the All-Powerful One is affected through the experiences, the actions, and the sufferings of Israel itself—that is, in God's essence, and not only in God's will. God's pathos has nothing to do with the whims of the mythical gods or with fate. God's pathos is a free relationship to creation, to God's people and their future. But it is also a relationship of passionate participation. The Eternal One takes humanity so seriously that God's Self suffers and can be wounded through humanity's sins. Certainly the images of Yahweh as a friend, as father, as mother, as disappointed lover of Israel, and the depictions of a zealous, jealous, angry, and love-hungry Yahweh are anthropomorphic images. But they are "God-commensurate" images. For they describe this one, unique passion of Yahweh for Israel, which Abraham Heschel called the divine pathos.

When Spinoza maintained that God could neither be angry nor love, he then fundamentally misunderstood this divine pathos. And when together with Greek philosophy even Jewish thinkers rejected these depictions of anger and passion as "God-incommensurate," they then threw the baby out with the bath water.

Abraham Heschel had shown that the prophetic experience of God could not be expressed through philosophical monotheism, because it is an experience of the divine pathos, not of the *Theos Apathes*. If it is correct to say that the human being develops his/her humanity in proportion to his/her experience of God, then one can follow Heschel when he contrasts the *sympathetic* human being with the Stoic ideal of the *homo apatheticus*. The experience of the divine pathos opens human beings for full love: they love with the love of God; they are angry with the anger of God; they suffer with the suffering of God; they rejoice with the joy of God.[5]

On the foundation of the Jewish basic experience of the divine pathos, Heschel then developed a *bipolar theology* of the covenant: God is at once completely free in Self and nevertheless committed in the covenant. God is the "God of all gods and the Lord of all lords" (Deut. 10:17) and nevertheless at the same time the covenant God of little Israel. "The Eternal One is enthroned, whose name is Holy . . . and nevertheless with the Lord dwells the lowly and humble of spirit" (Isa. 57:15). Heschel identifies, with exegetical evidence, the divine pathos with the *Ruach*, the Spirit of God. This bipolarity indicates a distinction in God: God the Ruler calls the prophets. The prophet becomes an *ish-ha-ruach*, a human being driven by the divine Spirit. If the prophet answers the call of the Ruler, then in truth the Spirit of God responds through the prophet to God's Self. Therein a self-distinguishing of God reveals itself.

Abraham Heschel has shown that the Jewish experience of God cannot be a simple monotheism, because on the basis of the experience of the divine pathos it must come to an awareness of this self-distinction of God. Every self-communication presumes a self-distinction. Whoever speaks of the communicability of God presumes a relationship in which God can step over against God.

These insights allow themselves to be deepened even further when we bring in the studies of the theology of the Rabbis by A. M. Goldberg[6] and Peter Kuhn.[7] What Heschel called "divine pathos" is here described as the "self-abasement of God." Ps. 18:36 is fundamental: according to Luther, "When you humble me you make me great," but according to Heschel it is "Your self-abasement shows me that you are great."

The history of the divine self-abasement begins with the creation and reaches on to the end of the world. God is always present in history in two ways: God abides in heaven, and with the widows and orphans (Ps. 146:6–10). God is sublime and looks upon the lowly. Like a servant God carries the torch before Israel wandering in the desert. Like a porter God bears the people with its sins. Thus God meets humanity in the lowly and in the small, in the despised and in the oppressed.

These *accommodations of God* to human history are however at the same time the *anticipations* of God's universal indwelling in creation, when God's glory will fulfill all things in the end. In God's Shekinah (condescension, indwelling) God is present in Israel, suffers with Israel, goes with Israel into exile, feels with the martyrs the agonies of death. "Since the suffering of God in exile was taken extremely seriously, the redemption of God's Self must also logically be perceived in the redemption of Israel from exile. . . . In this inner bonding through a common suffering God and Israel wait mutually for their redemption. Israel knows that it will be redeemed because God will indeed redeem God's Self and thereby also God's people. . . . The suffering of God is the *means* by which Israel will be redeemed. God's Self is the 'ransom' for Israel."[8]

This belief in the God who goes with Israel into exile is obviously the secret power which protects the people from despair and from numbness, and sustains in life its hope which is disappointed, embattled, and bombarded from all sides.

Because of the striking parallels, Peter Kuhn put forth the thesis that "primitive Christianity had used rabbinical presentations of the self-abasement of God that were already at hand in order to describe the incarnation and the passion of the Redeemer."[9] I am not able to evaluate this thesis historically. Systematically, however—that is, seen structurally—the commonality in the experience of the co-suffering of God and the recognition of the self-distinction of God in God's co-suffering is the most profound commonality that there can be between Jews and Christians.

And finally, to go a step further, I will present some reflections from Jewish mysticism. First of all Franz Rosenzweig:

> Mysticism bridges the gap between the "God of our Fathers" and the "Remnant of Israel" with the doctrine of the Shekhina. The Shekhina, God's descent upon man and his sojourn among men, is pictured as a dichotomy taking place in God himself. God himself separates himself from himself, he gives himself away to his people, he shares in their sufferings, sets forth with them into the agony of exile, joins their wanderings. . . . Nothing would be more

natural for the "God of our Fathers" than that he should "sell" himself for Israel and share its suffering fate. But by doing so, God himself puts himself in need of redemption. In this suffering, therefore, the relationship between God and the remnant points beyond itself.[10]

Also, according to Gershom Scholem, there is, "however many hesitations the mystics may constantly have in the face of this sentence, some kind of mysterious cleft, indeed not in the substance of the Godhead, but rather in God's life and works."[11] Now if this self-distinction of God and self-abasement in the Shekinah are the fundamental experience of Jewish faith, if this "cleft" in the life and works of God formed the experience of the Exile and of history, then what does "mono-theism" mean?

We have already shown that the axioms of philosophical monotheism—*apatheia* and *monas*—are not applicable to the Jewish experience of God. What then, however, is the deeper meaning of the Jewish confession of the One, Only God? In the historical experience of God, that is, in the exilic experience far from the homeland, as Franz Rosenzweig with extraordinary boldness wrote, the Shema meant "to confess God's unity—the Jew calls it: to unify God (*Gott einigen*). For this unity is as it becomes, it is Becoming Unity. And this Becoming is enjoined on the soul and hands of man."[12] The Cabalists also obviously understood the Shema in a similar way on the basis of "the exile of the Shekinah": "Only in the redemption, when the harmony of the worlds is restored, when all things take the place they should originally have had in the plan of the worlds, will—as the Bible says—'God be One and God's name be one' truly and finally."[13] The unity of God is, according to these Cabalistic presentations, an eschatological concept of hope which points to the redemption of the historical self-distinction of God. For this historical difference of God is precisely that difference in which the entire drama of history plays itself out. Therefore the redemption of history coincides with the redemption of God.

The experience of divine passion and the recognition of the

self-distinction of God revealed therein are therefore, I believe, Jewish possibilities.

If we return from this point to the Christian doctrine of the Trinity, then it will be immediately understandable that the passion of Christ is the basis for the Christian recognition of the Trinitarian self-distinction of God. "Not the spare Trinitarian formula of the New Testament, but rather the pervasive, consistent witness of the cross is the scriptural basis for the Christian belief in the triune God; the briefest expression for the Trinity is the divine deed of the cross in which the Father allows the Son to offer himself through the Spirit."[14] More precisely said, it is the offering up of Christ in the death on the cross which makes the Trinitarian self-distinction of God apparent and necessary in thought.

What happened on the cross on Golgotha between Christ and God, whom Christ always exclusively prays to as "my Father"? According to Mark and to Paul, Christ was "abandoned" by his heavenly Father: The prayer of Gethsemane was not heard, but rather was rejected. Jesus died with a cry and with all of the signs of being abandoned by God. The Greek word for giving over and abandoning—*paradidonai*—has first of all a clearly negative tone. It means to give over, to deliver, to betray, to reject.

In Pauline theology the term *paredōken* is first used as an expression for the now-revealed anger of God over the sins of humanity. In Rom. 1:18ff. *paredōken* three times indicates divine judgment: "And God gave them up to the lusts of their hearts." Humankind, which abandoned God, will be abandoned by God.

In a profoundly altered sense Paul uses the word "to give up" in Rom. 8:32, where he speaks of the abandonment of Christ on the cross in light of his resurrection through God: "He who did not spare his own Son but gave him up (*paredōken*) for us all, will he not also give us all things with him?" Thus God the Father gave up his "own" son, that is, abandoned, rejected, and gave him over to judgment, "for us," in order to give us "all things." Paul is still stronger in 2 Cor. 5:21: "For our sakes he made him to be sin"; and in Gal. 3:13: "He became a curse for us."

In the historical abandonment of the dying Jesus on the cross Paul sees the offering up of the Son through the Father, which was determined from all eternity. Because the Father "did not spare" his own Son, he does spare all the Godforsaken. Because he abandoned his own Son he becomes the Redeemer of all the Godforsaken. The Father loads the Godforsakenness of the Judgment onto his own Son in order to give to all the Godforsaken his grace and eternal presence. When Paul uses the *paredōken* formula, he always speaks of Jesus, of the "Son of God," never of Christ or of *Kyrios*, as if he wished to say that in the giving up and the abandoning of Jesus by the Father a cleft opens up in God which reaches so deeply that through it every cleft of sin and of judgment between God and humankind can be embraced and healed. The self-distinction of God embraces here not only the sublimity and the humility of God, it embraces not only the grandeur and the co-suffering of God, it embraces here the love of God and its opposite, the anger of God; the grace of God and its opposite, the judgment of God. The Trinitarian self-distinction of God in the death of the Son on the cross is so deep and so broad that all those lost and abandoned will find a place in God.

And yet further: in Gal. 2:20 Jesus himself is named as the subject of the giving-up. Paul speaks of "the Son of God, who loved me and gave himself (*paredōken*) for me." Thus not only does the Father give his only Son, but the Son also gives himself. The passion story of Jesus presents a passive and at the same time an active suffering of Jesus. The giving up of Jesus to the death on the cross is also a self-giving.

If one takes Rom. 8:32 and Gal. 2:20 together, then a conformity of wills between the Father who gives up his Son and the Son who gives himself up must be affirmed. This conformity is all the more astounding since the most profound separation between Jesus and his God and Father is nevertheless to be found in the Godforsaken death on the cross. The quotation from Ps.

22:2 is the only prayer in which Jesus addresses the Father with "my God" and not with "my Father."

As Rom. 8:32 and Gal. 2:20 show, Paul explained the abandonment of Jesus on the cross as a giving up, a giving up out of love. Johannine theology expresses this notion in the well-known sentence "For God so loved the world that he gave (*paredōken*) his only Son, that whoever believes in him should not perish but have eternal life" (John 3:16). By "so" the abandonment of Christ on the cross is meant, and by "he gave," the passion of Christ.

The First Epistle of John (4:16) sees in this event of the abandonment and giving up of the Son by the Father on the cross the very Being of God and captures this notion in the lapidary sentence "*God is love.*" Seen against the background of the history of the understanding of the New Testament this sentence means "God is Love" = "God is self-giving" = "Divine self-giving is this event on Golgotha": the Father gives the Son, the Son gives himself for us, and that happens through the Spirit (*dia pneumatos,* Heb. 9:14). In this event of the giving up "for us" lies the unity of the Trinitarian self-distinction of God.

The cross on Golgotha reveals the Trinitarian difference and the unity of God, for there the mystery of the triunity, which is open to the world, history, and humankind, is revealed. Conversely, however, one must then also say, "God is love," that is, "The Lamb who from the beginning of the world is slain" stands in the midst of the Holiness of the Trinity. God's essence is from eternity a love which is capable of suffering, ready to sacrifice and give itself up. This is for the Christian primordial experience the "divine pathos," the "self-abasement" of God, the prepared-for-exile Shekinah. There was a cross in the heart of God before the cross was raised up on Golgotha. In the death of the Son the eternal heart of the Trinity was revealed.

In the giving up of Christ on Golgotha God is not only revealed in history but also opened up to the experience of history. The history of the suffering of the world is the history of God's suf-

fering. The history of the conversion of humankind and its libera-
tion is the history of God's joy. However, if the Trinitarian God
is in the death of the Son opened to the experience of history,
then in view of this openness to the world its unity stands forth.
The Trinity does not wish to come to its own unity without the
comprehensive uniting of the abandoned and divided creation
with itself. God does not wish to attain eternal blessedness without the salvation of the image of God on earth. The more Christians grasp the passion of the Father which is revealed not only
in the cross of Christ but also is open to the suffering of the
world, that much more will they pray and hope for the unifica-
tion in the triune God. For only when the Son "gives over the
reign" (1 Cor. 15:24) to the Father will "God become all in all
things" and therefore "the One" in all things. Then will the Father
and the Son and the Holy Spirit be "the One and only."

In order to put the Christian experience of God in a series of
sentences, which is certainly inadequate, I would like to try to
say:

God is love.

God is self-communication.

Self-communication presumes self-distinction.

Self-communication fulfills itself in self-giving.

The love of God communicates itself to the other.

That is our freedom and our salvation.

Thus Augustine also related the doctrine of the Trinity to the
experience of the surprising, unmerited, and overwhelming divine
love:

> You see the Triunity
> When you see the eternal love;
> For the Three are the One loving,
> The Beloved, and their Love.[15]

To be sure, there are differences between Jews and Christians
in the experience and understanding of God. That fact should
not be flattened out as a result of this analysis. But after two
thousand years of deadly differences, the more profound con-

vergence may and must finally be brought out. In this the distinctions are to be affirmed as steps along the path to the recognition of one another and along the even broader path of hope with one another.

Abraham Heschel and Franz Rosenzweig, from whom I try to learn, were Jews. Paul and Mark, from whom I have received the gospel of the giving up of the Son of God "for me," were Jewish Christians. I myself am a gentile Christian. Those are three distinctions:

Christ has another face for gentile Christians than for Jewish Christians. For the latter he fulfilled the promises of their forebears, and thus showed to us the unending mercy of God the Father (Rom. 15:8–9). However, the gentile Christians are thankful to the Jewish Christians for their faith and their experience of God. And Jews became Christians not in spite of but rather because of their being Jews, as did Paul and Mark. Therefore, is not Jewish Christianity to be seen as a Jewish possibility? Is gentile Christianity not to be acknowledged as a Jewish-Christian insight and intention?

Because the giving up of the Jew Jesus, the Son of God, "for many" is the foundation of the Christian doctrine of the Trinity, the "Christian" doctrine of the Trinity also cannot be viewed as a contradiction to "Jewish" monotheism.

The experience of God and the knowledge of God by Jews, Jewish Christians, and gentile Christians converge in the common and unifying suffering of God and in the common and unifying hope in God, who is One and who will be One in all.

NOTES

1. Cf. Adolf von Harnack, *Lehrbuch der Dogmengeschichte*, 5th ed. (Tübingen 1931), 1:697–796; 2:304 (*History of Dogma*, trans. Neil Buchanan [Magnolia, Mass.: Peter Smith, Publisher]).

2. Aristotle *Metaphysics* 12. 1072b4–1073b14.

3. Abraham Heschel, *Die Prophetie* (Krakow 1936); *The Prophets* (New York: Harper & Row, Publishers, 1962), esp. pp. 221ff.

4. Heschel, *Die Prophetie,* esp. pp. 127–65 ("Die pathetische Theologie").

5. Heschel, *The Prophets,* esp. pp. 308ff.

6. A. M. Goldberg, *Untersuchungen über die Vorstellung von der Schechinah in der frühen rabbinischen literatur* (Berlin 1969).

7. Peter Kuhn, *Gottes Selbsterniedrigung in der Theologie der Rabbinen* (Munich 1968).

8. Ibid., pp. 89–90.

9. Ibid., p. 105.

10. Franz Rosenzweig, *The Star of Redemption,* trans. William W. Hallo (New York: Holt, Rinehart and Winston, 1970), pp. 409–10.

11. Gershom Scholem, *Die jüdische Mystik in ihren Hauptströmungen* (Frankfurt 1957), p. 253.

12. Rosenzweig, *Star of Redemption,* pp. 410–11.

13. Scholem, *Jüdische Mystik,* p. 253.

14. B. Steffen, *Das Dogma vom Kreuz: Beitrag zu einer staurozentrischen Theologie* (Gütersloh 1920), p. 152.

15. Augustine *De trinitate* 8. 12. 14.

Dialogue

LAPIDE: I wish to state the important matter first, for the forest comes before the trees, as the overview comes before the details.

For me Christianity is a God-willed way of salvation, and the church, if I may formulate it in Christian terms, is a valid structure of salvation. We Jews and Christians are and remain children of the One Divine Father, and our things held in common outweigh by far our legitimate differences. I say "legitimate differences," for I am absolutely convinced that God loves multiplicity and is the archenemy of Prussian uniformity. Otherwise God would not have so clearly written multiplicity into all of the natural sciences, into astronomy, into political science, and into biology, all of which indeed are likewise books of God, just as is the Bible. Consequently I believe in a plurality of ways of believing in the One God, and I am convinced that God is large enough that several paths of salvation could lead to God, of which Judaism and Christianity are only two. I believe, therefore, that our experiences of God indeed are different, as Moltmann says, but not so different from one another that it does not provide a broad basis for common further thought and for common reflection on God. Quite the contrary. I believe that it is precisely only the differences between us which enable our dialogic reflection to be truly fruitful.

Thus many of Moltmann's statements I can think along with him, and others I can feel along with him. That brings me naturally to the question which indeed is also the fundamental question of Moltmann as a believing Christian. I accept the resurrection of Easter Sunday not as an invention of the community of disciples, but as a historical event. For details I can only refer to my book *Auferstehung—ein jüdisches Glaubenserlebnis* ("Resurrection: A Jewish Faith Experience"). I attempt there in ninety-six pages to make this thesis of the historicity of the resurrection more or less clear. I am completely convinced that the Twelve from Galilee, who were all farmers, shepherds, and fishermen—there was not a single theology professor to be found among them—were totally unimpressed by scholarly theologoumena, as Karl Rahner or Rudolf Bultmann writes them. If they, through such a concrete historical event as the crucifixion, were so totally in despair and crushed, as all the four evangelists report to us, then no less concrete a historical event was needed in order to bring them out of the deep valley of their despair and within a short time to transform them into a community of salvation rejoicing to the high heavens. So much about the resurrection.

When I say that for me Jesus the Nazarene is immortal, I mean that in a twofold sense of the word: He is immortal in his visible, perceptible, and far-reaching influence—you Christians are the best evidence of this ongoing influence—through a community of salvation which spans all five continents. He is however also immortal since according to rabbinical teaching all the just who die for the God of Israel (and without doubt Jesus did) live on with God. How that happens we do not know. But that he lives on is for me a fact as much as that Rabbi Akiba, Moses, Abraham, Isaac, and Jacob are not ultimately dead.

I can therefore accept him as immortal without believing in his messiahship or in his sonship of God in the Greek sense, but I can believe in his sonship in the Hebrew sense, which is light-years away from the Greek, as we both know. That all brings us substantially closer.

When Moltmann says that the God of Israel is not an "apathetic" God who is incapable of suffering, who is enthroned high above in heaven without feelings, I am in complete agreement. For there is in the rabbinical literature an endless abundance of biblical texts and explanations of the Scriptures which speak of God as one who abases himself, who makes himself the servant of Israel and who suffers with his people. Out of this understanding there is also a Jewish doctrine which specifically connects the redemption of God with the redemption of Israel, indeed, which states that God wishes to redeem himself through and with Israel. These are things which are therefore infinitely distant from the feudal concept of a domineering God who despotically rules over his subjects. All that I can and will go along with. Because of Auschwitz I am almost forced to accept this "theopathy" if I wish to begin at all to incorporate the eclipse of God of the forties into my world picture and into my understanding of God, as for thirty years I have attempted to do.

I also understand it when Jürgen Moltmann says that for him the Trinity in no way begins with Nicaea or Constantinople, but that rather he understands it from Golgotha as the crucifixion event. Here the sentence that the Father gives himself over to (or *paredōken*, to rely upon, to give over) the Son through the Spirit serves as an example for me. But I do not perceive here the Trinity; that is not the correct word, because in my feelings and thoughts it does not appear to me as such. All my Jewish being speaks against it. All my life experiences, including Auschwitz, even if I was not there, forces me to a theological rethinking. I belong to the Auschwitz generation, which has to deal with the mass Golgotha of our days. As such I can sense this cruci-fixion—contradicting almost all rabbinical exegeses—as a kind of evidence of the self-sacrificing love of the divinity. It is not easy. However, what I find really difficult is the "separation of God from himself," which, as you rightly say, Rosenzweig maintains. It is difficult for me to grasp the notion that God divides himself. The famous citation of Isaiah, to which many mystics in Judaism refer (Isa. 57:15), literally concerns God: "I live in the heights [and in good English that means "transcendent"] and in the holy place [and that means "in the Temple of Jerusalem"] and with those who are oppressed and are of a contrite spirit." Here I can only say that this threefold indwelling of God, which, however, so completely eludes all human logic, melts into a unity in the faith world of Judaism. We know of no contradiction between the

immanence and the transcendence of God; we know of no contradiction between prayer and command, between ethics and
mysticism. For the God who dwells in the highest heavens and
was present in the holy place, as long as it still stood, and at the
same time proclaimed to the contrite God's being with them, is
for me not a divisible God, or as Rosenzweig said, a God of self-
distinction. God is the Incomprehensible One, so that our tiny
human brain cannot comprehend this All-Unity and therefore
divides it into two or into three. That is not only Christian; it is
true also for certain circles within Judaism, which go as far as
ten. The Cabalists have a ten-level theology. That strikes normal
Jews like myself as illogical, and precisely therefore, perhaps, it
also belongs in the faith world of Israel.

In other words, when I re-present to myself Golgotha, then the
God who suffers through the son—one of his sons—the God who
loses this son and thereby experiences infinite pain, and all of this
so to say through the spirit, is one and the same God. For this
spirit of God for me is not hypostatized and has no special existence, but in good Hebrew fashion it is an emanation of God, in
other words, a radiation of the One God, and is as integral a part
of God as, for example, the word of God, the love of God, or the
mercy of God. I could indeed, according to this logic, as a Jew
go further and hypostatize the mercy of God and make of it a
special existence. For me that would be almost blasphemy. For
me this God with all the various attributes is the One and the
Only, and if I cannot grasp that with my human intellect, so
much the worse for my brain. But because of God's incompre-
hensibility I am still not prepared to divide God into two or
into three or into ten so as to make God more easily presented.
Thus my head often stands in contradiction to my heart, but in
matters of faith my heart has the last word.

MOLTMANN: It is always a joy to speak with Dr. Lapide, whether
it is in dialogue or in disputation, because gentile Christians always have dimensions of their own faith tradition newly opened

to them through the presence of a Jew, and especially an Orthodox Jew. It has become clear to me, which was not earlier the case, that there is an existential difference between being a gentile Christian, a Jewish Christian, and a Jew. Presumably the triumphalism of the church had in earlier times clipped all persons with the same comb and shears, and therefore demanded the same from all of them. Consequently I have said that Jesus has another face for Jewish Christians than he does for gentile Christians, and in this I have depended upon Paul. That is also true for Jews. What for us as gentile Christians is not possible to think of in another fashion—because we are only able to experience it through the gospel, which comes to us as a pure grace—must not be the same for Jews, because they have another approach to the gospel and it meets them in another way. Indeed, the same God need not show the same face to everyone, for in fact God has made everyone different and Jews and Gentiles have had a different history. To become conscious of one's own existence, with its limitations and its possibilities—to learn that—is very important.

Now, however, concerning our common problems: I have above all in the reading of Abraham Heschel noticed how very much our concept of God is determined by Greek monotheism. It is a dogma for theology and a tradition of our church that God cannot suffer. This understanding was taken over from Greek thought and has become a general presupposition. Divine nature is incapable of suffering. From this results, then, the difficult problem of the two-nature Christology: the divine nature is incapable of suffering, the human nature is capable of suffering. But what then really happened on the cross? I will not now go into the details and the possible solutions of this problem. Abraham Heschel makes it clear that Judaism in Europe, from Maimonides to Spinoza, likewise proceeded from the axiom of God's incapability of suffering, so that the insight that the God of the Old Testament not only is projected anthropomorphically but in fact is also a "jealous God"—and that this may not be done away with if one

63

wishes to retain the original experience of God—is a new discovery. In this connection our common, far more difficult problem is to comprehend the unity of God, while the description of the experience of God and the speaking out of the experience about God appears to me to be a far less difficult problem.

The unity of God appears to me to be the greatest mystery. No, I certainly do not wish to know more than Dr. Lapide knows. I wish only to make an effort to remove that which in my—gentile—mind stands in the way. Already in the translation of the Shema Israel we have several statements: God is One, God is the only God, God is God alone, an All-alone God. Perhaps there are still other possibilities to express the unity which God is and which we confess. However, they must all be distinguished from the *monas* of numerical unity as the foundation of all mathematical concepts. Numerical unity is indeed itself no number but is the foundation of all numbering. The numerical figures two, three, four, five, and so on always proceed out of numerical unity. One must not hold up before Christians the notion that they would have a multiple God if they did not understand God as a monarch and if they reject the concept of numerical unity as the mystery of God.

You have said that it is difficult for you to think of the self-distinction of the One God without thinking of a division of God into several parts. My dear Dr. Lapide, if God is indivisible, then how can God communicate God's Self? Must we not leave behind the concept of unity as the smallest indivisible particle and utilize another concept of unity if we proceed from the communication, the self-communication of God, and then also—as I believe—from the self-distinction of God?

The doctrine of the Trinity certainly has not hypostatized the attributes of God so that one could have three or even ten. Its beginning point lies much more in the event of the self-distinction of God which allows God to communicate God's Self, to go about with Israel, and to suffer on the cross of the Son. The unity of God is to be thought of in the self-distinction of the Father and the Son. It is the Holy Spirit who presents the unity in this self-distinction. When you speak of emanations instead of hypostases, then you are very much in the line of the Neoplatonic speculation: there one finds triads and thousandfold emanations. But the *self*-distinction is not thereby at all comprehended. Certainly our difference also lies in a linguistic difficulty. You have indicated that with the reference to the contradiction between your heart and your head; but my gentile head has still more difficulties than your Jewish head in the understanding of the biblical God.

LAPIDE: You are right when you say that if I were to view God as a static unity, there would be no self-communication of God. There is a very ancient midrash, which Jesus certainly knew, concerning the cardinal question of the Rabbis, Why did God create the world? What purpose did God have for it? The answer of the scribes, after hundreds of years of reflection, was as follows: God created it out of love. Why out of love? Because love is the only thing which has need of a partner, and therefore God created humankind in God's image. God created something that is like unto God; that is what we all are, but we are in no way the same as God, just as man and woman are similar to each other but, thank God, are not the same. This comparison is not related in jest; it stems from the rabbinical heritage. Thus a God who was not communicable could not really be a Jewish God, because we Jews see this world really only theocentrically, but we experience our God really only anthropocentrically. We know of no "God in self." That is a God of the philosophers in Greece. An "aseism" is unknown to us. We can only experience a God who gives himself to us to be known anthropocentrically. Hence all the Jewish attributes of God are oriented toward the human person. What then are kindness, grace, mercy, and love, if not anthropocentric attributes because thus and only thus can we experience God, without thereby wishing to say that we have herein—God forbid—exhausted God's entire essence. That would be blasphemy indeed! Nevertheless, only thus can we experience God—through God's manner of revelation—as for example God's kindness, mercy, and love.

Since we therefore do not wish to know anything of a rigid, static monotheism, the bridges between us ought not to be all that difficult to build. They would only have to stay away from the philosophical Trinitarianism of the first church councils: The work of a school of extraordinary Greek theologians, or better said, Greek philosophers, who only shortly before had been baptized and who did as Augustine did when, with captivating openness, he said that he had substituted for the philosophy he had until then a "better philosophy," namely that of Christianity. We must gain a certain distance from these gentlemen for whom Jesus the Jew was essentially alien and return to Golgotha, for that was still primordially Jewish—both as an event and also in its original interpretations. Primordially Jewish Jewish-Christian is for me still Jewish. There perhaps we can find a starting point which, to close with Blaise Pascal, is not the God of the philosophers but rather truly the God of Abraham, Isaac, and Jacob. There most probably a dynamic monotheism would be formulated, as Moltmann has defined it: A God who suffers with us even unto the death of the cross and gives himself over, as he perhaps delivered himself at Auschwitz, as he starved with his Jews in Treblinka, as God who gives himself over in a self-willed powerlessness, and out of limitless love. That would be a presentation of God—far from rigid monotheism, which once was nothing other than a reaction against pagan polytheism—which I would be prepared to think through again anew in the sense of a God who manifests himself in the plural reality; a God who communicates himself, and therefore also hopes for his realization in humankind; a God who in his creaturely image can suffer, even unto death; a God who wishes to suffer with and love with in the double meaning of "sympathy," who also wishes to live out before us in suffering an "Imitatio Dei."

That, perhaps, might be the direction of a bridge between us.

MOLTMANN: No, that *is* the bridge, not just a road sign to the bridge, and it is not only a theoretical bridge. To build the bridge from the Jewish to the gentile shore and the reverse can certainly take place only in the experience of a common suffering. I say that although I belong to the people who have caused your people unending suffering, and therefore stand entirely on the other side. But it is imaginable, and I expect it, that Jews and Christians one day will undergo a common persecution and then will discover the redeeming love of God that binds them at the most profound level. That then is the bridge. One does not need to build it. It is already there from eternity. But will Christians and Jews then recognize it and walk on it?

AUDIENCE QUESTION TO LAPIDE: What prevents you then from having yourself baptized and becoming a Christian? You confess the Son of God, and hence it is a contradiction if you do not become a Christian.

LAPIDE: I believe in "sons of God," as Jesus (Matt. 5:9; 5:45) and Paul (Rom. 8:14) described them; an "only begotten Son of God" I do not know. Concerning baptism, I must state that everything which I have until now learned about Christianity has strengthened and undergirded my being a Jew. One thing, however, we Jews and Christians should not forget: concerning the first and the last things both of us know as good as nothing. We *believe* with the rock-firm conviction of the heart, but neither of us can logically prove the fundamentals of our religion. Humility is therefore the first commandment for all participants in every authentic faith conversation. That Jews and Christians can walk together until Good Friday is in my opinion only a partial truth; I believe we can remain together until Easter Monday and even conceive of the resurrection in Jewish terms, but not as the eschatological watershed, as you do, as the "center of time," as Conzelmann calls it. I see it plainly and simply as a historical event, as a tangible reality, as an indication for the primitive community that this Jesus was not abandoned by God, as a kind of response to the words, troubled unto death, which were spoken on the cross: "My God, my God, why have you forsaken me?" I accept the resurrection in the sense that, I believe, the primitive community understood it. However, I cannot accept it as an eschatological beginning, as an inbreaking of the Reign of Heaven, because unfortunately I am unable to discover a single trace of this Reign of Heaven.

QUESTION: If the resurrection was a historical event, why then did the Jews not react to it? For the resurrection could certainly be accepted by believing persons!

LAPIDE: If the resurrection of Jesus from the dead on that Easter Sunday were a public event which had been made known to, according to my counting, not only 530 Jewish men and women, but could have been experienced by 530,000 Jews (approximately the then-current population of Jerusalem, which was swollen by the stream of Passover pilgrims), a crossroads in salvation history would have been arrived at. Do you know what would have happened then? I can imagine only the following happening: all Jerusalem would have become believers in Jesus—for do not forget that Messiah is a Hebraic concept, that "Messianitis" was and is a Jewish illness (namely, the almost feverish expectation of the Redeemer), and that no land in the world and no city under the sun awaited the Redeemer in such yearning fashion as did Jerusalem during the lifetime of Jesus. If he had shown himself as the Resurrected One, not only to the 530 Jewish witnesses but to the entire population, all Jews would have become followers of Jesus. To me this would have had only one imaginable consequence: the church, baptism, the forgiveness of sins, the cross, everything which today is Christian would have remained an inner-Jewish institution, and you, my dear friend, would today still be offering horsemeat to Wotan on the Godesberg. Put in other words, I see in the fact that the Easter experience was imparted to only some Jews the finger of God indicating that, as it says in the New Testament, "the time was fulfilled." For me that means that the time was ripe that the faith in One God should be carried into the world of the Gentiles. The Jews were already believers! They were already on the way to God. Or as Rosenzweig so beautifully put it when he accepted the sentence of John, "No one comes to the Father except through me!" (John 14:6), no one except those who are already with the Father, and those are the Jews. And if you Christians for fifteen hundred years were wont to explain the parable of the two sons such that the son who remained home is the Jew while the lost son who wandered off to the Gentiles is the church, who then penitently comes back home, where the Father embraces him full of love despite all his sins and his previous godlessness and commands that the fatted calf be slaughtered for him, then please also be so logical as to read the next sentence out of the mouth of the father, who can be no one other than God the Father. "My child," says the father to the son who remained home (that is, us Jews), "You are always with me, and everything which is mine also belongs to you!" (Luke 15:31). Hence, I do not need the Christ in order to come to the Father.

In other words, I believe that the Christ event leads to a way of salvation which God has opened up in order to bring the gentile world into the community of God's Israel. Above all, three things were necessary for the founding of the gentile church to which you belong (as a Jew I am thinking now in a historic-pragmatic, three-dimensional fashion): First, a Jewish people in its biblical homeland in order to bring Jesus and the apostles into the world. Secondly, there was needed a small Jewish yes to Jesus—that is the primitive community, together with Paul and his helpers. Finally, however, there was also needed a large Jewish no. For if there had been no large Jewish no, which you can read about in Romans 11 and in Acts 13, the entire church would have remained intra-Jewish—and to be honest, we did not need it. Since Sinai we have known the way to the Father. You on the other hand were very much in need of it. Therefore, your becoming Christian is for me a portion of God's plan of salvation, and I do not find it difficult to accept the church as an institution of salvation. But please, you do not need to sprinkle sugar on top of honey, as you do when you wish to baptize us. The sugar on top of the honey is simply superfluous. We are already "with the Father" and we know the way, despite all the sins, stiff-neckedness, and transgressions of which we are guilty and which we penitently confess. We are certainly no saints. We are not even just. But we are Jews, who know the way to the one Father. It is similar to, if not identical with, the way which Jesus of Nazareth and, after him, Paul of Tarsus opened up and showed you.

MOLTMANN: Theological thought is always conceived within a history, not only in the matter which is reflected upon but also in the form in which it is thought. What you have spoken of as dualistic thinking has an old tradition indeed, if thereby you mean the Platonic dualism of idea and reality. However, there are also other traditions. What you refer to as polar thinking is really dialectical thinking, as Hegel, above all the young Hegel, understood as the thinking of the living: one must think of the living in a living manner and one may not kill it through definitions and domination. Therefore one must attempt to raise up the existing oppositions into polar tensions so as to overcome their destructiveness. Then these tensions will become creative and fruitful for life. I maintain that today this is an urgent task of thinking and judgment—where usually mutually exclusive opposites are left to stand, which then lead to the death of the other side.

In this regard the Old Testament is for us Christians an extraordinary training in thinking. I do not wish thereby to say that as gentile Christians we ought only to live from the Old Testament words and presentations, but rather that we be schooled in the understanding of reality by the Old Testament form of expression, of narrating the history of God, and the experiences with God. Gerhard von Rad has shown many theologians the way to make the Old Testament, and no longer just Nicaea and Chalcedon, a thought-school for the understanding of the New Testament. This, of course, says nothing negative about Nicaea and Chalcedon, or concerning a freshly converted "band of philosophers," as Dr. Lapide is wont to express it. Ultimately everyone must do with their own gifts what they can to honor the One God. Why not philosophers with that which they have learned from Plato or Aristotle?

LAPIDE: Jesus, who as a devout Jew in Jerusalem was crucified by the Romans, was, according to my historical knowledge, one of thousands. Just as before Jesus, so also with and after him only all too many suffered a rebel's death. Remember, three crosses stood on Golgotha. Three Jews hung on them. Also, after Jesus historical reports speak unambiguously of thousands upon thousands of crucifixions of precisely the most devout in Israel, who because of their belief, sometimes because of their Zealot belief but always because of their belief in God, were crucified by these gentile Romans. The only unique element in the crucifixion of Jesus is for me its history of effects, the like of which there is not. In his name, and only in his name, was this world-embracing *Ecclesia Christi* founded, and I would be the last to view that as a side issue. I must honestly state that I will never be finished with this fact of the founding of the church, which sprang from the crucifixion. That is, I know the end of my thought process, namely, that the coming-to-believe of Christendom was without doubt a God-willed messianic act, a messianic event on the way to the conversion of the world to the One God. I do not know, however, how I should fit that into my spiritual framework, into the thought structures and faith categories which I have inherited from my fathers. But that is my difficulty. The end result I know with certainty. How I shall reach there I do not yet know. But I hope to think still more on the matter.

Was all that an erroneous path, did the church not go false there? Absolutist claims and salvation monopoly are un-Jewish concepts—at least since Malachi. I believe, however, that since

71

Isaiah we acknowledge a multiplicity of paths of salvation, and the Talmud says three times, "The non-Jew who concerns himself with the teaching of God is made equal to the high priest in Jerusalem." In order to bring the absurdity of this Jewish statement home to you I will translate it into Catholic language: The Jew who reads the New Testament (as I do, for example) is made equal to the Pope in Rome in his claim to salvation. What would be a poor joke in Rome was already two thousand years ago in Jerusalem a biblical truism. Therefore, I cannot think that there is only one path of salvation, because for me that would come to the same thing as a blasphemous diminution of God, for God is much too great for there to be only a single path of salvation to reach God. With the prophets of Israel I say that there are many God-willed paths of salvation, not only those of Christianity, Judaism, and Islam. Outside of these three classical paths of salvation there must be still others, because the God of our forebears is a God of the universe and, as it says in the First Letter to Timothy, in good Jewish fashion, "God desires that everyone be saved" (1 Tim. 2:4)—a wonderful biblical truth which is as Jewish as it is also Christian. Therefore, God cannot condemn six hundred million Chinese to hell, nor God knows how many hundreds of millions of Hindus, Brahmans, and Buddhists. Indeed, not even the Communists are lost, without salvation. *How* God will accomplish that escapes my mind. But *that* God wishes it and can accomplish it belongs to the bedrock of my Jewish faith.

For me *messiah* is not such a terribly reserved and exclusive word which one must lock inside a monstrance. In my Hebraic Bible there are at least six different messiahs. David was one, Saul was a second, Solomon a third, even the idol-worshiping gentile emperor Cyrus was, according to Isaiah 45, a "messiah of the Lord." And in Qumran three different messiahs were awaited daily. The Talmud knows at least two: one messiah the son of Joseph, and another messiah the son of David, so that the concept messiah is not the alpha or the omega of salvation history.

Or perhaps we could formulate it thus: we Christians and Jews are two types of messianic religions. Said otherwise, redemption is for us the unrelinquishable part of belief. The difference is only in how we perceive this messianism. With you the king stands in the middle, and with us it is the kingdom. With you the redeemer, with us the redemption. Thus, in the Middle Ages after centuries of absurd forced disputations, which a triumphal church forced harassed rabbis into for the sake of the entertainment of the masses in the marketplace, it went so far that in the disputations with the Dominicans, for example, about "Christ in the Talmud," Joseph Albo, one of the outstanding figures of Judaism, clearly renounced his belief in messianism as a foundation stone of his faith. How could he do that? Quite simple. He referred to the words of Isaiah, repeated five times, which are said in the name of God, "I am the Lord, the Redeemer of Israel, and there is no other!" (Isa. 43:11). In other words, however you view messianism, from a Jewish view it remains at bottom only an instrumentality. For the one who ultimately redeems is God alone. What instrument God makes use of for that purpose is God's business. For us the main thing is the redemption itself, whose result is rather clearly described in Isaiah 2 and Isaiah 11. Whoever as the anointed one of God brings all this to pass is at bottom for us of secondary concern. That God and God alone can accomplish it is for us a self-evident matter.

MOLTMANN: [A response to a comment by the host Lutheran pastor.] May I attempt to respond in a few words. You have, pastor, left something out. You have left out *to whom* God wishes to reveal God's Self through Christ. When you take the addressee into consideration, you must distinguish between Jews and Gentiles. Dr. Lapide has earlier presented in salvation-historical terms what Paul in Romans 9—11 says about the role of Israel. Paul spoke of the "hardened hearts," Dr. Lapide spoke of the "large no" of Israel. The gospel came to the Gentiles. With an eye to the Gentiles it has taken on this form which reaches us and which calls us.

There have always been Christian attempts to locate Israel in God's plan of salvation, either in such a way that the church replaces Israel as the new people of God—and thereby tendentiously liquidates Israel—or in such a way that Israel is recognized to have a further vocation of salvation alongside the church, for God is true and remains true to the promise to the people of God's choice. In this latter case one views the church and Israel alongside of one another until the day of which Paul says, "What will their acceptance mean but life from the dead?" (Rom. 11:15).

From Dr. Lapide we have received for the first time an answer to the question of the salvation-historical significance of Christendom in a Jewish perspective. I find that wonderful. I can accept it: Christendom is the *praeparatio messianica* of the gentile world for the Reign of God. That of course does not conversely mean that Israel now is already in the Reign of God, to which the Gentiles only now should come; a relationship of Israel to the Reign of God, for which the gospel prepares the Gentiles, is to be thought out in a much more separate fashion. It is something that you must work out with your hope and with your God and not with us. Is not Israel itself also a *praeparatio messianica*, even if incomparable, for the Reign of God?

I see the matter thus: Israel and Christendom are moving on the same path, but with different tasks. Their union into oneness will be brought about only in messianic time in the fullest sense of the word, in the Reign of God. Then also will the special calling of Israel be fulfilled, and when the Reign of God comes in its glory and everyone worships the One God, the existence of the church will also be superfluous.

LAPIDE: When Moltmann says that I see Christianity (and thank God, I am not the only Jew who does so) as a *praeparatio messianica*, he takes the words right out of my mouth. I believe that that is also christologically digestible, for the Christology of the New Testament is neither eternal nor final. It is clearly given a time limit by Paul and is up till now preeschatological; therefore, it exists before the fulfillment of the final times. Two things make possible a partial bridging over of Christology, which makes a rapprochement possible. The first is that the Reign of Heaven is not yet there, but has only been initiated—a view which I perhaps could accept. The second is that Christ will not sit at the right hand of the Father for all eternity, as it states in your credo, coming from Psalm 110, but that one day he will return the lordship to the Father and then the Father again will be "all things in all" (1 Cor. 15:28), which appears to correspond to the prophecy in Zech. 14:9.

Jürgen Moltmann wrote of a "Hebrew wave" which is now passing through Christian theology, after Greek thought more or less had come to an end. I believe he is correct. I also feel something of the pulse of the zeitgeist in present-day Protestant theology. If we wish to break through to that real Jesus who led the West to One God, we must return *ad fontes* of Israel, and part of this today includes the dismantling of these in-between stations of the Greeks which could have been necessary for salvation in the early Middle Ages. For without Nicaea, Constantinople, and the church fathers there probably would have been no universal church— that is correct.

Otherwise the primitive church probably would have remained a Jewish sect. All that is correct and true. But what in the first and second centuries encouraged the faith through thought structures and patterns of speech which were adapted to the zeitgeist of that time, at the end of the twentieth century has the far-reaching effect of being discouraging to faith. Sometimes I visit Protestant and Catholic seminaries in order to speak with the twenty- and thirty-year-olds as representatives of the church of tomorrow. They choke badly on the Greek formulas, as, for example, from Chalcedon, and the Creed of Nicaea and Constantinople. Some choke so badly that sometimes I fear that they might throw out the baby with the bath water because they are not prepared to bring a *sacrificium intellectus* to every worship service, that is, to offer up their human understanding on the altar of their faith. They say rightly that their understanding is also God-given, and God could not demand that they should three times a day give up their understanding because the formula of faith demands it of them. Once, twice, yes, but certainly not every day. Thus it appears to me that this return to the primordial Jesus who lived, strove, and died in a very non-Greek way, which the zeitgeist in present-day Christianity appears to be striving for, will perhaps lead to a Christianity in the twenty-first century which will correspond more to the attainments of technology, science, and our new knowledge of the world, will respond more wisely to the faith needs of human beings and will demand less sacrifice of our understanding in the word-for-word parroting of the Greek formulas of salvation which were vital fifteen hundred years ago but today are ripe for the museum.

Said in other words, I accept Jesus as a believing Jew who had a central role to play in God's plan of salvation and in whose name a worldwide church was founded. I do not believe that in God's plan of salvation, as far as I dare to divine it—of knowing it there can be no talk—a charge was given to him to lead Israel to God. In my opinion that would have been a superfluity. However, I am not relativizing the matter, and I sense between your lines that that is a suspicion: if there is a multiplicity of paths of salvation which lead to God, then at bottom it is a matter of indifference whether I take the Christian, the Muslim, or the Jewish path. I in no way say that. I believe that I as a Jew should follow the Jewish path, and I am no less convinced that as a good Christian your only path is the Christian one. I do not believe, however, that I should become a Christian or that you should become a Jew. I believe that we must maintain our two separate existences alongside of each other, exactly as we maintain the fact that in biology there is a kind of inexhaustible multiplicity so that even two Siamese twins are not identical with each other, to say nothing of all the human beings under the sun.

The conclusion is unavoidable: God wishes this plurality and perhaps also wishes that we strive toward God along different paths of salvation—all the more so since these paths of salvation indeed have a half-dozen cardinal things in common: the One God, the hope for salvation, a large part of the Bible, and not least, the teleology of history, that is, that we know that our history has a goal and a meaning. In other words, we believe in a causal beginning of this world, in a goal-conscious further movement, and in an end full of blessing; all three things we believe—in a kind of salvation-historical "triunity." We likewise believe that the prophets spoke in God's name. We also both believe in Jesus, only we evaluate Jesus differently. Do you not believe that these broad commonalities are strong enough to maintain a side-by-side relationship and to justify a common reflection such as we are engaged in today without each one insisting that his way is the only path of salvation?

MOLTMANN: According to Käsemann, however, salvation concerns the title of Christ, not the title of the Son. Christ's lordship reaches from his resurrection up to the time that he gives the Reign over to the Father. So long is he *Kyrios*. When he gives over the Reign to the Father his lordship ceases, because then the greater Reign takes its place. But as 1 Cor. 15:24 shows, the title of the Son remains: Jesus gives the Reign to the Father. Here the same expression appears which also described the obedience of the Son: *hypotassesthai*. I believe that Paul employs the title of the Son whenever he speaks about the relationship of Jesus to God his Father, whereas he uses the title of Christ and of *Kyrios* in order to express the significance of Jesus for humanity. But that is my suspicion. Otherwise one would have to—as Emil Brunner insisted—conceive the doctrine of the Trinity only as the teaching of a historical self-distinction of God; then at the end there would be the *hen kaip an*, that is, the mystical thought which allows everything finally to be taken up into the one God.

I would like once again to come back to the question of the perception of one's own existence. Eugen Rosenstock-Huessy once said there are no human beings, there are rather only Jews, Christians, and pagans. That is in any case a salvation-historical description. And if for me as a gentile Christian Jesus is the Son of God who reveals to me the grace and mercy of the Father, then for gentile Christians it looks exactly as I now am attempting to describe it. For Jewish Christians it appears differently, because for them the fulfillment of the promise of their forebears is involved, who indeed are not my forebears, for I am a gentile Christian. Therefore for Jewish Christians the gospel appears somewhat differently, and for Jews who have not become Jewish Christians and have good grounds for that, even good salvation-historical grounds, it looks different still again. I can well imagine that some Orthodox Jews would see in Jesus their brother, a believing Jew, and thus respect him in an appropriate manner, while for me as a gentile Christian Jesus is the Redeemer, the only Messiah, for my history knows no such series of messianic pretenders of whom Dr. Lapide spoke. Therefore for me Jesus is the only path to salvation. How Israel deals with its own future, the Reign of God, and sets itself in relationship to its own genuine future, that is an Israelite question. I would therefore, when I read the New Testament together with Jews, like to proceed from Romans 9—11, and I am very sorry that you do not take Paul in Romans 9—11 completely seriously, my dear pastor, when you do not wish to affirm a legitimate Jewish no to the messianism of Jesus. Paul called the no of Israel "a hardening." Does one have a free choice with a "hardening"? The very same Paul also described the responsibility of the Christians toward the Jews: not to missionize them like the gentile peoples—for Israel is not a gentile people—but rather "to stimulate them to faith." But that, however, is something quite different from insisting that they must accept everything in the confession of faith of the gentile Christians. On this level I can understand myself as a Christian and also the Jewish partner.

LAPIDE: Two things. First, when I say that I do not need Christ, that is meant as a path of salvation; for when I previously said that in his name the world church was founded, which for me is an indispensable in-between station to humanity's becoming believing, in this sense I do need him—only perhaps not so immediately as you need him, because for me he is not needed to prepare the path to the Father. When you speak of "the sonship of God," I am happily prepared to go along. However, I have a condition, which is scientifically fair: in the mother tongue of Jesus. I preferably read *Faust* in German and Shakespeare in English. Therefore let Jesus speak in Hebrew and Aramaic. There the sonship of God means something completely different, namely, in the meaning of Matt. 5:9: "Blessed are the peacemakers, for they shall be called the *sons of God.*" Or Rom. 8:14: "All who allow themselves to be led by the spirit of God are the *sons of God.*" In this sense—and I have still another six similar quotations from the New Testament—Jesus was without doubt a son of God. But when you counter me that he is the only-born son of God, I can only respond that in Exod. 4:22 God says to Pharaoh—the God who is the Father of Jesus Christ—"Israel is my firstborn son." And since that can be documented to have taken place over a thousand years before Jesus, Jesus of Nazareth can in the best case be called only the second-born son of God. I wish to end with this citation from Jürgen Moltmann. On page 139 of his book *The Church in the Power of the Spirit* (New York: Harper & Row, Publishers, 1977) it says: "Through his crucifixion Christ has become the Saviour of the Gentiles. But in his parousia he will also manifest himself as Israel's Messiah."

I find in this sentence an acceptable formula of reconciliation. For until God grants us certitude, this hope shines its light—*sub conditione messianica!* In other words, since no Jew knows who the coming messiah is, but you believe to know his identity with certitude, I cannot contrapose your certainty with a no, but merely with a humble question mark. Thus I am happily prepared to wait until the coming one comes, and if he should show himself to be Jesus of Nazareth, I cannot imagine that even a single Jew who believes in God would have the least thing against that. We trust in the salvific action of God blindly and without question. Should the coming one be Jesus, he would be precisely as welcome to us as any other whom God would designate as the redeemer of the world.

If he would only come!

The Quality of the Messiah

MOLTMANN: Christianity and Judaism have developed themselves separately in history. Because in the beginning Judaism, but later also Christianity, did not wish to recognize the other side but did everything to suppress it, consequently those areas which are life necessities for Jews and Christians were also suppressed in our originally common hope. Because Christianity arose out of the belief in the Messiah Jesus and lives in this belief, the original expectation of a messiah in person was pushed to the background in Judaism behind the expectation of a messianic time. And because in Judaism the hope for the Reign of God was dominant, the originally realistic expectation of the Reign of God in Christianity was pushed back behind that salvation which was already brought through Christ. Whoever on the basis of belief in the Messiah Jesus still hoped for that greater Reign was branded as having "Judaizing tendencies." Therefore Schalom Ben Chorin was right when he said, "In general it can be said that while for Judaism the Reign overshadowed the messiah, in the church Christ overshadowed the Reign."[1]

Because these one-sided elements arose from the history of the conflict, they must be overcome in the present rapprochement between Jews and Christians. For Christian theology there arises the task of placing Christology and eschatology in a relationship in which the one no longer "overshadows" the other, but rather enlightens it. The Christian "cult of personality" with the Messiah will be overcome when the person and the history of Jesus are perceived and understood within the future horizon of the judgment and the Reign of God. We call this "eschatological Christology." With it the church recognizes that it is not yet the Reign of God, but its herald and sacrament. If the church recognizes its own precursor character in relationship to the coming Reign, then it can and must acknowledge Israel as a partner and preparer of the way for the Reign alongside of itself in history. Anti-Semitism and persecution of the Jews always arose from the identification of the church with the Reign of God. Then Christology became set absolutely and no Jewish existence in its own hope was permitted.

Because christological absolutism and ecclesiastical and Christian triumphalism can be said to be overcome, might these familial questions of Christians likewise be put to the Jews: What do you think about the messiah? Must the overshadowing of the messiah by the Reign of God remain? When, as Dr. Lapide has impressively presented, the Jewish faith awaits redemption from God alone and therefore the coming messiah can have only an instrumental significance, what relationship has God then to the coming messiah and what relationship does he have to God? Is not the thought of election implied in the thought of his "instrumental significance"? The coming messiah is, however, this one and no other—this one whom the election as the instrument of divine redemption has marked out? Is not a unique relationship of God to the messiah contained, then, in this election? And if this should be so, must not this unique relationship of God to the coming messiah and of the messiah to God also be described with unique concepts which are to be applied only to him, with names and concepts which are not to be applied to every member of the people of God in like fashion? Certainly the coming messiah can only be a member of the people of God itself, but nevertheless, he also stands as an instrument of redemption over against the people in the name of God. How will that be expressed? The Christian messianology—I choose this expression in order not always to speak of Christology, since the title Christ has long since become for many Christians a proper name of Jesus—has brought to expression the two-sidedness of the "instrument" of the redemption: the messiah is the redeemer for humanity and the chosen son of God. He is for God, who communicates himself in the redemption, the "only-born son." He is for the redeemed the "firstborn son" from among "many brothers" and sisters. Could these not also be possibilities for a Jewish messianology, when the awaited Reign of God shall no longer "overshadow" the messiah, but enlighten it?

LAPIDE: In the eschatological thinking of Israel the messianic bringer of salvation is a latecomer of the second temple era. Isaiah described the reign of peace in the final days in brilliant colors, which have need of no mediator between God and humanity (Isaiah 2). On the contrary, repeatedly the herald in Jerusalem set forth the word of God: "Fear not, you little worm of Jacob. . . . I will help you, says the Lord, and your Redeemer is the Holy One of Israel" (Isa. 41:14). "I am your God and the Holy One of Israel, your Savior" (Isa. 43:3). "I am the Lord, and beside me there is no Savior!" (Isa. 43:11).

The Hebrew Bible of Jesus and his brothers knew of the messiah only as a priest (Lev. 6:15ff.), as a prophet (1 Sam. 2:35), or as a king (2 Sam. 19:22), a multiplicity of offices which enabled David to speak of "the anointed ones" of the Lord (Ps. 105:15).

Only in Hasmonaean times, as the gruesome yoke of the Gentiles and the failure of their own leaders brought the people to the edge of despair, did there arise from the abyss of suffering a vision of an anointed redeemer who as an ideal regent embodied truth and justice, and who was destined to restore the order of God in a world that had fallen out of joint. This worldly function of bringing about the Reign of Heaven is so closely bound up with his urgently yearned-for coming that in almost all of the manifold presentations which are woven around his figure, he was and is awaited as the "messiah king."

That his coming was considered necessary is reflected by the realism which in view of the corruptness of political forces on earth has been dominant in Judaism since time immemorial. The certitude of his ultimate advent rests on the unshakable faith in

God's continuing concern for creation. The firmness of the hope in the inbreaking of God—thanks to which the messiah will accomplish the liberating redemption from need and death, from suffering and covetousness, from hunger and war—is the primal ground of that indestructable optimism of the Jew which could survive even Auschwitz.

Prince of Peace, Offspring of David, Good Shepherd, Light to the Gentiles, Anointed Warrior, "Like unto a Human," Comforter, "Firstborn," and a "Son" of God—all these and a dozen other names of honor and titles of respect are nothing other than the many-voiced expression of that Jewish yearning, which will not be quieted, for redemption, which melts the saving will of God, the messiah, and the Reign of Heaven into such a powerful future hope that it constantly incites us to an impatience which is thirsty for salvation, which can approve of no today, nor canonize any status quo.

The common elements in the many-colored palette of Jewish messianic expectations are the messiah's divine charge to bring about the promised redemption in the public showplace of world history, and his being in the image of God, as are all his fellow human beings, which permits him as the chosen one of God to come as close to his Creator as we all are allowed to—and not one step closer.

Thus all messianic speculation in Judaism remains "functional" rather than "personal," for all believing Jews pray daily *for* the messiah—no one prays *to* the messiah. This instrumentality of the redeemer king enabled several of the outstanding figures of the medieval rabbinate, when faced with the forced disputations of a triumphal imperial church—which attempted to prove its redeemed character with all the means of power—to give up the faith in the messiah as a foundation of Judaism. Indeed, in the vortex of the militant Christomonism of the Church authorities there even developed a kind of Jewish antimessianism which could say:

"After the enslavements in Egypt there came the redemption

through Moses. After the enslavement by Babylon there came the redemption by Daniel, Hananiah, Mishael, and Azariah. After that came the persecutions by Elam, the Medes, and the Persians, and the redemption by Mordecai and Esther.

"After that there came the enslavement by Greece and the redemption through the Hasmonaeans and their sons, and then there came the Roman captivity. Then the Israelites said: We are tired of being redeemed and enslaved, redeemed and again enslaved. We want no more 'redemption' by human hands. Redemption comes only from God" (Midrash Tehillim on 36:10).

Thus Christianity step by step became a who-religion, whose fundamental question about the essence of the Godhead was: *Who* is the Creator of the universe? *Who* is God's Son? *Who* is the true Christ?

Judaism on the other hand was and remains predominantly a what-religion, which forgoes the profoundly probing who-question and pragmatically hopes to determine *what* God has accomplished on earth, *what* corresponds to God's will, and—in the most daring case—*what* God intends for us.

This who-what debate, which naturally cannot be corralled in any precise schema, often reminds Jewish readers of the New Testament of the dispute between the two hills, between the hill of the Sermon on the Mount in Galilee and the hill of Golgotha in Jerusalem—between the *what* Jesus proclaimed in his eschatological message and the *who* of his person as the christologically proclaimed one.

Judaism and Christianity are both stamped with a profound messianism. The former, however, places its emphasis on the *what*: the redemption. The latter on the *who*: the redeemer himself.

That the who and the what are not to be separated here, indeed that "both are the words of the living God," as the Pharisees were careful to say in their disputes, is evidenced both by the second petition of the Our Father, "Your kingdom come!" and also the twelfth truth of faith of Maimonides, which has long since become part of the liturgy of the synagogue: "I believe with complete conviction in the appearance of the messiah, and even if he tarries I will nevertheless daily await his coming."

NOTES

1. Schalom Ben Chorin, *Die Antwort des Jona* (Hamburg 1956), p. 109.

The Positive Meaning of the Jewish No to the Messiahship of Jesus

LAPIDE: "You have rejected the Savior!" Thus since the early Middle Ages was the "Christian" excuse expressed for the most debased inhumanities which have ever been performed in the name of a religion of love.

Also on the theological level most Christians have made it all too easy for themselves: the Redeemer of the world is already come and has performed his saving work, they maintained, so that now belief in him is sufficient in order to ensure everyone the attainment of salvation. Because the overwhelming majority of the Jews refused to recognize this version of the plan of salvation, a whole series of angry reactions were forthcoming, which found their theological expression already in the New Testament. Compressed into a single sentence, the answer of the early church was expressed in one of its foundational dilemmas:

Since Jesus worked his whole life long as a Jew among Jews and for Jews, which Jews nevertheless rejected him as Savior, these Jews therefore must be either spiritually blind and hardened or devilishly evil—probably both. Since every other answer appeared to shake the foundation pillars of the Christian saving truth, this ingenious solution was undergirded, widened, and believed with industry and imagination from the first century onward.

Jesus was ever more clearly in the writings of the church anointed the Messiah of Israel; ever more raucously did his rejection by "the Jews" ring; ever more shrill sounded the casting aside of Israel placed in the mouth of Jesus, so that in the devel-

opment of the *apotheosis* of Christ every elevation of the Nazarene appeared to demand a further humiliation of his people.

What unites all these primitive anti-Judaisms of a mentally lazy
gentile world is the claim to know precisely the counsels of God:
a broken relationship with the Bible of Jesus and with his primordial church, the fusing of the salvation of Christians with the con-
demnation of the Jews, and not least, an almost two-thousand-
year-long consequential history which yoked together Jesus-love
and Jew-hate in an antibiblical pair.

From the Jewish side anger called forth counteranger, which,
however, almost without exception expressed itself only in battles
of words and vilifying writings.

Already in the high Middle Ages the fury of a biblically con-
ditioned reflection softened so that there was a recognition in
the Christian yes to Jesus of a coming to believe in the God of
Israel. Indeed, the greatest thinkers of the Spanish Diaspora saw
in Christianity, which brutally persecuted their fellow believers,
a "preparer of the way for the messiah king."

Friedrich-Wilhelm Marquardt begins his essay on "Enemies for
Our Sake" (Rom. 11:25ff.) with the words, "We will have placed
Christian anti-Judaism behind us only when we have theologically
succeeded to begin to do something positive with the Jewish no
to Jesus Christ" (*Harder Festschrift,* 1977, p. 174).

Do you see a possibility of taking up this suggestion and dis-
cussing it?

MOLTMANN: I will very gladly take up the suggestion of Friedrich-Wilhelm Marquardt. The gospel of Christ would never have
reached the nations of the world, and that includes us Gentiles,
had not Israel as a whole and through its official representatives
spoken a no to the proclamation of Jesus as the promised Christ.
Christianity would have remained an inner-Israelite messianic-
awakening movement and would have oriented itself only toward
the reestablishment of the twelve tribes of Israel, as this was sym-
bolized in the twelve apostles. According to the prophetic vision,

the history of salvation should run: first the Jews, then the Gentiles. When Israel is reestablished as the people of God, then the Gentiles will make a pilgrimage to Zion in order to find there justice and righteousness.

The community of disciples which gathered around the twelve apostles remained within their own people. Indeed, they did not exclude proselytes from among the Gentiles, but they did, however, exclude an active mission to the nations. Only with the rejection of the gospel by Israel as a whole, which specifically did not exclude individual Jewish Christians, but rather whose existence it included, did that terrible turning about of the prophetic vision of the history of salvation come forth from those Jewish Christians who gathered themselves in the circle around Stephen and the Apostle Paul. On the basis of the rejection by Israel as a whole, salvation by the gospel went first of all to the Gentiles: the last shall be first and the first last. According to Romans 9—11 Paul is convinced that Israel as a whole will convert when the fullness of the nations have been won for Christ. "The mission of the apostle is a fantastic detour on the way to the salvation of Israel" (E. Käsemann). Through Israel's "fall," as Paul expresses it (Rom. 11:11), the Gentiles attained salvation, so that Israel would emulate them. Therefore Paul commends his office as the "apostle to the Gentiles" in order "to make my fellow Jews jealous, and thus save some of them" (11:14). The apostolate to the Gentiles and the church of the nations are, in the complex paths of the history of salvation, necessary detours to the salvation of Israel. The internal basis for the gospel which is open to the world is the giving of Christ for the reconciliation of the world. The external occasion for the gospel being proclaimed throughout the world is the rejection by Israel as a whole.

For a gentile Christian, then, speaking not too precisely, there is nothing more positive for his salvation than the Jewish no. However, one can say that only if one knows that there is nothing more positive in the world for Israel's salvation than the faith in Christ of the Gentile. The faith of the Gentile is the detour to the salvation of Israel: not so that Israel should accept the Christian faith and be able to enter into the Christian church. Precisely not that! But rather so that Israel might more passionately believe in *its* God and hope in *its* salvation the more it sees the faith of the Gentile and the hope of Christendom.

Thus must it be theologically seen. However, precisely because of this must one sigh under the wretched burden of guilt for Christian anti-Judaism. Whoever said, or still says, "You have rejected the Savior," hates not only the Jews but also the Savior and at bottom hates himself. Whoever said, or still says, "Israel is nothing other than one among many nations which has no special significance for the history of salvation," despises not only Israel but also the Lord and therewith the foundation of his own salvation. Whoever says, "Israel was once the people of God; now, however, Christendom is the people of God," declares Israel as antiquated and passé; such ones have no hope for Israel and at bottom also have no hope for themselves.

Christendom can gain salvation only together with Israel. The Christians will one day be asked, Where are your Jewish brothers and sisters? The church will one day be asked, Where have you left Israel? For the sake of the Jew Jesus there is no ultimate separation between the church and Israel. For the sake of the gospel there is provisionally, before the eschatological future, also no fusion. But there is the communal way of the hoping ones.

A Common Declaration

The tragedy of Christian-Jewish relations lies above all in the fact that Jesus of Nazareth, who should have been "our peace" (Eph. 2:14)—a bridge of reconciliation between Israel and the world of the nations—has become a trench of hostility.

"You will be hated by all nations for my name's sake" (Matt. 24:9).

However one wishes to exegete these words of Jesus, the fact is that it literally describes the almost two-thousand-year history of separation between the brothers of Jesus and his disciples—in crass contradiction to the Sermon on the Mount, the great command of twofold love (Mark 12:28–34), and to the Jewish heritage which was the spiritual *Sitz-im-Leben* of the Nazarene.

When the teacher and the (later) teaching, the preaching and the praxis separate from one another so terribly, when the good news of the Christians could become the sad news of the Jews, we should pluck up our courage so as to place before us the basic questions:

Is the separation of our paths, this living apart from one another by two familial faith communities, justified in the saving will of our heavenly Father?

Where is it really the Lord, the Eternal One, our God, who separates us in all that which for so long a time has split and alienated Christians and Jews? And where is it we, with our handiwork and our human thoughts, who set up barriers and hinder a rapprochement?

Three times in the Old Testament and three times in the New Testament it says, "Upon the testimony of two or three witnesses will every matter be verified."

Several witnesses are needed, then, who are of a mind to give testimony jointly and in agreement; not, however, who argue with one another, pile up contradictions, or indeed attempt to defeat one another. How then shall this God-alienated, revelation-blind world believe our testimony of the gracious love of God if we give the lie to one another, live past one another without contact, and sing hallelujahs against one another?

Can we in the house of prayer say yes and amen to the promised Reign of Peace—only to deny the reconciliatory will of God by our deeds?

Just as our earth has become much too small for the ambitions of hostile superpowers, so is the infinite God of the universe much too large for the monopolistic claims of self-glorifying salvation chauvinists.

A common earth under one Father-God—this global imperative does not demand any artificial unifying of all paths of faith, but rather a unity in plurality, in the expectation of that day in which "all nations will call upon the Lord with one voice in order to serve shoulder to shoulder" (Zeph. 3:9).

We should live in this concord as an example to our splintered, self-torn world, for only then will our confession of the God of the Bible be accepted as true.

That is the challenge to our faith today. Here lies the touchstone for the new dialogue between Christians and Jews.

It has already grown late. The time on the world clock presses.

Half a century ago Martin Buber dreamed in Stuttgart: "If Judaism would again become Israel . . . the division would probably remain undiminished . . . but there would not be a sharper exchange between us and the church. Rather something completely other would come forth which today is still indescribable."

Perhaps he meant a genuine two-way conversation of an open faith to an open faith, of a love-filled seeking and finding, of a taking of the other seriously and of a joy in our twoness which only in God knows a oneness.

What is needed for such a dialogue? Three things—nothing more:

—a "listening heart" as Solomon once requested (1 Kings 3:9);
—the humble insight of Paul that all of our thinking, doing, and speaking remains "imperfect" (1 Cor. 13:9ff.);
—and the understanding of the universal message of the Bible that God "wants everyone to be saved" (1 Tim. 2:4).

To the never-ending search for truth—which knows that no religion is an end in itself or an island, but only a pilgrims' path to God—these building stones for a biblical bridge are dedicated.

JÜRGEN MOLTMANN   PINCHAS LAPIDE